SAMS
Teach Yourself Today

e-Auctions

e-Auctions

Bidding, buying, and selling
at eBay and other online auction sites

Preston Gralla

201 West 103rd Street, Indianapolis, Indiana 46290

Sams Teach Yourself e-Auctions Today

Copyright © 2000 by Preston Gralla

International Standard Book Number: 0-672-31819-9

Library of Congress Catalog Card Number: 99-067010

Printed in the United States of America

First Printing: December 1999

01   00   99   4   3   2   1

Trademarks

All terms mentioned in this book that are known to be trademarks or service marks have been appropriately capitalized. Sams Publishing cannot attest to the accuracy of this information. Use of a term in this book should not be regarded as affecting the validity of any trademark or service mark.

Warning and Disclaimer

Acquisitions Editor
Jeff Schultz

Development Editor
Ned Snell

Managing Editor
Charlotte Clapp

Senior Editor
Karen A. Walsh

Copy Editor
Pat Kinyon

Indexer
Amy Lawrence

Team Coordinator
Amy Patton

Interior Design
Gary Adair

Cover Design
Jay Corpus

Copy Writer
Eric Borgert

Production
Dan Harris
Staci Somers

Table of Contents

Acknowledgments

Thanks to acquisitions editor Jeff Schultz for trusting me with this book and for helping shape and guide it in its earliest days so that it was on-target. And thanks to all the good folks at Macmillan USA: Development Editor Ned Snell, Project Editor Karen Walsh, Copy Editor Pat Kinyon, Indexer Amy Lawrence, Proofreader Charlotte Clapp, and Layout Technician Staci Somers.

As always, thanks to my agent Stuart Krichevsky, my wife Lydia and my two kids, Gabriel and Mia. Gabe and Mia, in particular, helped by helping participate in auctions themselves. Lucky kids—they came out of it with extra Pokémon cards and PlayStation games bought from auction sites.

Foreword

Visit an auction site such as eBay on any given day, and you can just feel the energy. It's the energy of the millions of people who pass through the site regularly to buy or sell just about anything you can think of, from an autographed Darth Vader helmet or "LBJ for president" matchbook to — for the next two hours only—a rare copy of the Japanese release of Donny Osmond's hit "Go Away, Little Girl" in its original sleeve.

No matter how obscure the item, if you find it at all, you'll find it at an e-auction. That's why auction mania has hit full force on the Net.

The online auction is one of the greatest inventions to come from the Internet so far. I say this because it embodies the very things that make the Internet the powerful medium that it is: a global meeting place, a source of vast information and, in turn, a dynamic commerce tool.

Online auctions bring millions of people together in a virtual open-air market, where Joe in Phoenix can buy that rare collectible from Jane in Kalamazoo, or Berlin, or Reykjavik, for that matter. Sellers, whose businesses often thrive from the comfort of home, can display their wares 24 hours a day, for the whole world to see, not just the folks in town.

But where does one begin learning how to buy or sell on these mammoth sites? This book gives you the lay of the land, whether you plan to buy or sell, or just observe the fast-moving action on these sites. As we at *Access Internet Magazine* know, people want to hear how stuff on the Internet works, without all the jargon. Preston Gralla does just that here, explaining, in laymen's terms, what types of auctions exist, how to properly buy and sell, and how to protect yourself, from beginning to end.

I know for a fact that the warnings that Preston mentions should be taken seriously. If only I'd had a book like this before making my first e-auction transaction a few years ago, I'd probably have a poster of the film "The Third Man" hanging on my wall, instead of a $50 lesson to beware of scams.

This book is filled with useful tips that will prepare you for the world of e-auctions. It's a fast-growing, fast-paced world, so hold on tight, remember the advice you read on these pages, and let the bidding begin.

Stephanie Chang

Editor, *Internet Access Internet Magazine*

www.accessmagazine.com

INTRODUCTION

Every day, thousands of people are buying long-lost treasures or everyday goods at bargain rates, are making a substantial amount of money selling goods they no longer want, and are having fun while they do it.

They're participating in a one-time craze that has become a way of life for many people—online auctions, also called e-auctions. At e-auctions, people buy and sell through an auction Web site, and what can be bought and sold is limited only by the imagination. Collectibles, such as Beanie Babies, stamps, coins, glassware, movie posters, jewelry, and everything else that has ever been collected; computers and home electronics; household goods; cars... just think of something, and it's been sold via an e-auction.

Even tickets to Fenway Park for the long-anticipated playoff showdown between the Boston Red Sox and New York Yankees were sold via e-auctions—to the tune of $12,000 a ticket (peanuts and Cracker Jacks not included).

For many people, though, e-auctions may be a bit intimidating. They might not know how to bid or how to put something up for sale. They might be worried about dealing with strangers, or concerned that they'll pay for something and it won't be delivered. Or they worry that they'll overpay for an item.

As I'll show you in this book, it's easy to participate in online auctions and to do it without worrying that you'll do something wrong or get taken for a ride. I'll teach you everything you need to know to buy and sell online. You'll learn not just the basics of buying and selling, not just the mechanics of how you participate in auctions. I'll teach you smart techniques, auction secrets, and great strategies for becoming a pro in no time.

There are many online auction sites, and many more popping up each day. The biggest one is eBay, but there are many others as well. In this book, you won't learn just how to bid and buy on eBay, but on any auction site on the Internet.

So whether you want to buy and sell at e-auctions, merely dip your toes in and give it a try, or immerse yourself in online auctions, I'll show you how to buy and sell at online auctions. You'll learn how to find bargains, beat other bidders, and make money by making a sale—and you'll have fun along the way, just as I did when I first learned how to use e-auctions.

How to Use This Book

I've organized this book into six parts. As you go through them, you'll get an introduction to e-auctions, learn the basics of bidding and buying, learn how to put your items up for sale (including strategies for finding great stuff to sell!) and complete the deal as a seller, find out how to protect yourself at auction sites so that you won't get burned, and get a listing of the many other auction sites online.

In Part 1, "Online Auction Basics," you'll learn benefits of using online auctions, find out the different kinds of online auction sites, and learn auction basics. In this section, I'll teach you the basics of bidding, buying, and selling, and will give you an understanding of the different types of auctions, such as proxy auctions and Dutch auctions. At the end of Part 1, you'll explore the biggest auction site of all—eBay—and learn how to get started buying and selling there.

In Part 2, "Being a Savvy Buyer," you'll learn everything there is to know about bidding and buying at e-auctions. I'll start off by teaching you how to browse and search at auction sites to easily find the exact items you want to buy. Then you'll see how to check out a seller before bidding on an item and go through a buyer's checklist—a list of things you should always do before making a bid. After that, I'll show you how to actually make bids—and I'll give you auction secrets for making sure you win at auctions at the prices you want. You'll find out how you pay for items and get them shipped to you, and you'll learn how to keep track of all your bidding and buying.

In Part 3, "Auction Marketing 101," I'll show you how to become the auctioneer—how to sell items at e-auctions. You'll first find out how to create basic auction listings. Then I'll give you inside secrets about how to create auctions that sell—how to write auction copy that draws in bidders, how to use HTML to create eye-catching auctions, and how to add pictures to your auctions. Additionally, you'll learn a variety of other tips, such as knowing which days of the week and times of the year are best for selling things online. And I'll show you all the places you can buy inexpensive items that you can turn around and sell for a profit at e-auctions.

Part 4, "Completing the Deal," shows you how you'll receive payment from the highest bidder, and how you'll ship out the goods after you get your money. I'll teach you how to make contact with the high bidder and close the deal once the auction closes. You'll learn the best way to accept payment, and finally, I'll clue you in on the best ways to ship the goods to the highest bidder.

In Part 5, "Caveat Emptor," I'll teach you all the ways to make sure that you don't get burned at e-auctions. You'll learn how to check out bidders and buyers before participating in auctions. You'll get a list of things that you shouldn't buy at auctions, and you'll find out what you can do if you ever do get burned. I'll explain how to use escrow services—third parties that accept your payment and then release the money to the seller only after you receive the items in good shape. You'll learn about auction insurance that covers you should you ever get burned, and how to use appraisal services to make sure collectibles really are what they're claimed to be.

Part 6, "Appendixes," will be a useful reference for you in the months to come. In Appendix A, "Auction Web Sites Directory," I'll give you a comprehensive listing of the best auction sites on the Internet, so you can begin bidding, buying, and selling not only on big sites like eBay, but on sites that specialize in certain kinds of items, such as coins, Beanie Babies, or sports cards. Appendix B is a glossary that defines all the terms you'll need to understand to get the most out of online auction sites.

Let's Get Bidding and Buying!

So, we're done with our introductions. Now it's time to dive into the book. As you read it, you might want to hop onto the Internet and check out the auction sites as you read. So come on along. Get ready to bid and buy!

PART 1

Online Auction Basics

CHAPTER 1

Why Use Online Auctions?

Online auctions are the hottest thing on the Internet these days, and with good reason. If you're a buyer, you can find great deals on everything from computers to coins to Beanie Babies to jewelry and almost anything else you can imagine. And if you're a seller, you'll be able to make money in your spare time—you may even turn selling on auctions into a full-time business.

In this chapter, you'll learn what an online auction is, you'll get a basic understanding of how online auctions work, and you'll find out all the reasons you should use an auction site. You'll get a basic understanding of what online auctions are and why you should use them.

What's an Online Auction?

You're no doubt familiar with real-world auctions. In real-world auctions, an auctioneer has something for sale and puts it up for bid at an auction house or other location. People come to the auction house and bid against each other on an item. The highest bidder wins. Only the high bidder pays—unsuccessful bidders don't spend any money if they lose.

An online auction is similar in many ways to real-life auctions. Someone puts an item up for bid, and then people try to outbid each other to buy the item. But in this case, sellers and bidders don't go to a physical auction house. Instead, they go to a Web site where bidding takes place, such as eBay, pictured here.

What You'll Learn in This Chapter

► Exactly what online auctions are, and how they're similar—and different—from real-life auctions.

► The lowdown on how online auctions work.

► The basics of how to find items to buy on an auction site—and how to bid on them.

► The basics of how you can sell items at an online auction.

► All the reasons it's worthwhile to use auction sites.

Larger than any auction house in the real world, eBay is the world's largest online auction.

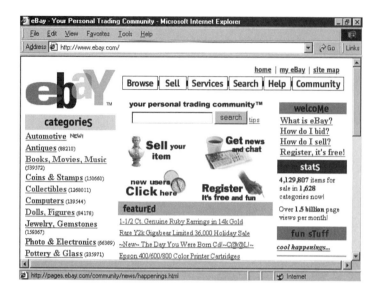

As in real-life auctions, only the high bidders pay for and get the items they're bidding on. Low bidders don't pay.

But while real-life and online auctions are basically similar, there are a lot of differences as well. The differ in the following ways:

Note:

When you buy from Web sites rather than individuals, you may get a warranty, and you'll usually be able to pay by credit card.

- *In most online auctions, you buy directly from the seller*—In traditional, real-life auctions, you buy from an auctioneer. Not so in most e-auctions. In most online auctions, you don't buy from the auction site. Instead, you buy from an individual. The auction site, in these instances, merely serves as a kind of broker, getting buyers and sellers together. As you'll see later in this book, though, you buy directly from the auction site at some Web sites, not from an individual.

- *In most online auctions, the auctions last for days, not merely for several minutes*—Unlike real-life auctions, the bidding at online auctions isn't "live"—it takes place over a long period of time, and bidders don't have to all be there at the same time. Bidders look at the highest bid, make a higher one if they want, and then check back again in hours or days to see if someone has made a higher bid. An exception is a "flash auction," which is done live over the Internet and lasts for a short period of time. Flash auctions are not that common. Turn to Chapter 3, "Understanding Auction Basics," for more information about flash auctions and other kinds of auctions.

- In online auctions, you can't examine the goods ahead of time—In real-life auctions, you can usually examine the goods before you buy. You can't do this in online auctions. Instead, you depend on reading the auction listings—in essence, an online auction catalog.

- *In online auctions, the buyers and sellers have to arrange for the goods to be shipped privately*—At online auctions, the buyer and seller have to make arrangements with each other for shipping the goods via the mail or delivery services. Usually, but not always, the seller pays for shipping. For information on shipping, turn to Chapter 10, "Getting the Goods When You Win," if you're a bidder, and Chapter 19, "How To Ship Your Items," if you're a seller.

How Online Auctions Work

In the previous section, I briefly described how online auctions work. Here, I'll go into a bit more detail. First we'll look at how you buy things at online auctions, and then at how you sell them.

How You Buy at Online Auctions

When you go to an auction site and you're out to buy, the first thing you'll usually do is browse the listings. Typically, items will be listed by category, such as Coins and Stamps or Collectibles. Each category is divided into subcategories, so it'll be easy to find the kind of item you're interested in. You can also type in a word to describe the kind of item you're interested in buying, such as *Confederate coin*.

No matter how you find an item you want to buy, you'll end up on a page that describes what's for sale. You'll find a description of what's for sale and sometimes a picture of the item as well. On many auctions, there is also a minimum bidding price, and you'll see the current high bid as well. Pictured next is part of an auction page on eBay, and part of one on Amazon.com.

For More Information:

There are literally hundreds of auction sites on the Internet. For a list of many of the top auction sites on the Internet, turn to Appendix A, "Auction Web Sites Directory."

Here's where you'll find information about an item for sale and do the bidding—an auction page on eBay.

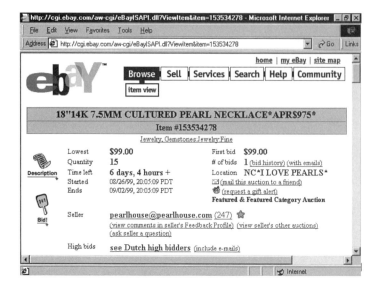

Here's an auction page on Amazon.com.

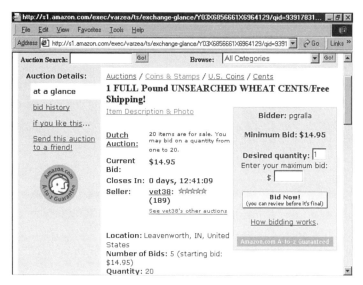

Here's where you'll do the same thing done in the preceding figure, but this time on Amazon.com auctions. If you're interested in bidding on the item, you enter your bid by filling out a form. (Before bidding or selling, you'll first have to register at the site.)

Each auction runs for a specific amount of time, two weeks, for example. During that time, people continually come by and bid, so you'll have to keep checking back to see if anyone has bid higher than yours—and to enter an even higher bid if you still want the item at the higher price.

At the end of the auction, the high bidder and the seller are notified via email of each other's email addresses. Then it's up to them to make payment and shipping arrangements. Many sellers ask for some kind of guaranteed form of payment, such as a money order or certified check.

There's a lot more to the bidding process, but that covers the basics. For more information about bidding, turn to Part 2, "Being a Savvy Buyer."

How You'll Sell at Online Auctions

When you want to sell something at on online auction, it's generally a simple matter. Determine a minimum selling price (or decide that there's no minimum price, and that you'll accept *any* bid), decide in which category your item should go, and then fill out a form that details what you have for sale. To make the item more enticing, you can add pictures, fancy fonts, and other extras to your auction page. You'll have to pay the auction site for your listing—and the fee is usually based on the selling price of what's up for sale. Keep in mind that even if you don't sell the item, you'll still have to pay the auction site.

At the end of the auction, you make arrangements with the buyer for payment, and then ship the goods. Again, there's a whole lot more to the process—to learn more about it, turn to Part 3, "Auction Marketing 101," and Part 4, "Completing the Deal."

Why You Should Use an Auction Site

So by now you have a basic idea of how auctions work. But there's an even bigger question that needs answering— why bother? Why spend the time at an auction site? What are the benefits?

The buyer should pay for the shipping

While there are no absolute rules about who pays for shipping costs, it's customary for the buyer to do so. So when creating your auction listing, make sure to specify that the buyer will pay for shipping—and detail exactly how much the shipping costs will be.

After you start buying and selling at auctions, you'll find there are a whole lot of benefits. The following are the most important:

- *You'll save money*—For many people, this is the biggest benefit of all. You'll spend less money at auction sites than you will buying the same goods at a store, and sometimes there are huge bargains to be had.

- *You'll find hard-to-find items and collectibles*—In search of an Indian head Pez dispenser? How about a *Godzilla* movie poster from the 1960s, rare Beanie Babies, or any other of tens of thousands of items? You won't find them near home or in retail stores. You *will* find them at auction sites—and easily.

- *You'll be able to make extra money*—One man's trash is another man's treasure. Next time you're cleaning out your attic or garage, don't throw away what you find—there's probably something you have that someone else wants to buy. It's easy to make money at auction sites, as you'll see throughout this book. It's so easy, in fact, that people have been able to make their living selling through auction sites.

- *It's a great way to join a community*—Online auctions aren't only places to do business—they're places to make and meet friends as well and join in a worldwide community.

- *It's just plain fun*—Looking for hard-to-find items, finding treasures all over the Internet, outbidding others in sometimes fast-and-furious action—online auctions can be a great form of entertainment.

Going, Going, Gone!

Online auctions are among the most popular sites on the Internet. Before you head to a site, you need to know the following:

- At most auction sites, such as eBay, you'll buy from the seller, not from the site itself.

- Online auctions don't occur in "real time"—instead, they occur over a period of days or even weeks as sellers check into the site and bid against one another.

Note:

When you make money by selling items at auctions—and especially if you make a living at it—you're supposed to pay income taxes on your sales, so keep track of your earnings.

- At the end of the auction, the seller and high bidder are notified via email. It's then up to them to make arrangements for
  payment and shipping. Typically, sellers ask for a guaranteed
  form of payment, such as certified check or money order.
  Usually, buyers pay for the shipping costs.

- Sellers have to pay the auction site to have a listing there.
  The payment is usually based on the selling price of the item.
  Even if an item doesn't sell, the seller has to pay the auction
  site fee.

- Auction sites will save you money and help you find hard-to-
  find or rare items. As a seller, they're also a good way to
  make extra money.

CHAPTER 2

What Kinds of Online Auction Sites Are There?

Before you head to an auction site and start making bids or putting things up for sale, you first need to know what kind of auction sites you'll find on the Internet. In this chapter, you'll learn about the different kinds of auction sites, and you'll find out what you need to know at each site before bidding.

Understanding the Different Kinds of Auction Sites

Here's some good news for you potential auction hounds: There are hundreds of auction sites where you can buy millions of different items. Now here's the bad news: With so many different kinds of auction sites out there, it can be quite confusing to know how to bid and sell at each one.

The best first step to learning how to use all the auctions on the Internet is to understand the different kinds of auction sites out there and what rules apply at each. The following are the main kinds of auction sites you'll find on the Internet. In the rest of this chapter, I'll cover them in more detail, teaching you the basics of what you need to know at each before bidding and buying.

- *Auction sites where you buy from individuals or companies, not the site itself*—At these sites, the auction site serves merely as a broker, getting buyers and sellers together. It may provide other services, such as auction insurance to make sure that people don't get burned from buying there, but it's up to the buyer and seller to complete the deal—the site doesn't get involved other than to get buyers and sellers

What You'll Learn in This Chapter

- ▶ Auction sites in which you buy from individuals or businesses, but not from the auction site itself.

- ▶ Auctions in which you buy directly from the auction site itself.

- ▶ eBay, which isn't really a separate kind of auction site, but is the world's biggest online auction. At eBay, you buy from other individuals, not from the site itself.

- ▶ Auction sites that specialize in a certain kind of item, such as stamps or military memorabilia.

together and inform each who the high bidder is. The most well-known example of this kind of site is eBay, but there are many others as well, such as the auctions held at *Amazon.com* and *Yahoo.com*.

Tip:

Before you buy directly from an auction site, make sure it's reputable by looking for contact information, a postal address, a phone number, and similar information.

- *Auction sites in which you buy directly from the site itself—* At these sites, you're not buying from another individual— instead, the auction site itself does the selling. Often, at these sites, you're buying new goods. At sites where you buy from individuals, the items are often used, rare, or collectible. The prices at sites where you buy directly from the site often aren't as low as at sites where you buy from other individuals. However, when you buy directly from the site itself, you can usually pay with a credit card, which affords you some kind of consumer protection. These sites often offer warranties on some products. The *www.firstauction.com* site is an example of one where you buy directly from the site.

At some e-auctions, you buy from the site itself, and at others from individuals

Before bidding, it's important to know whether you're buying from the site itself or from an individual. If you're buying from the site, you'll want to look for things like warranty information. If you're buying from an individual, you'll want to check out the buyer. But at some sites, you'll sometimes buy from the site and other times from an individual. So always know exactly from whom you're buying before bidding—never make any assumptions about who's doing the selling.

- *Specialized auction sites*—Sites like eBay sell everything under the sun. But there are also hundreds of sites that specialize in specific items for sale, such as coins, sports memorabilia, and crystal. If you're a hard-core collector of specialized items, it's worthwhile to check these sites. Keep in mind, though, that a big auction site like eBay also has many of these specialized items for sale.

We'll cover each of these in more detail in the rest of the chapter.

Auction Sites Where You Buy from Other People

As I've mentioned before, at the most popular auction sites on the Internet, such as eBay and the auction sites at Yahoo! and Amazon.com, you don't buy from the site itself. Instead, you buy from other people—or sometimes from businesses who are selling things at auctions. Either way, though, you're not buying from the site itself.

At sites like this, there are a number of things you have to keep in mind before bidding and buying. The following is a list of what to know and do before bidding and buying at these kinds of sites:

- *Check out the seller before bidding*—Most auctions sites, such as eBay, let people rate sellers as to how reputable they are. Before bidding at an auction site where you buy directly from an individual or company, you should check out a seller's rating. On eBay, click a link just below the seller's name to see the ratings. Pictured next is an example of what you'll see when you check out a seller. For more complete information about how to check out a seller before bidding, turn to Chapter 6, "Checking Out a Seller Before Bidding."

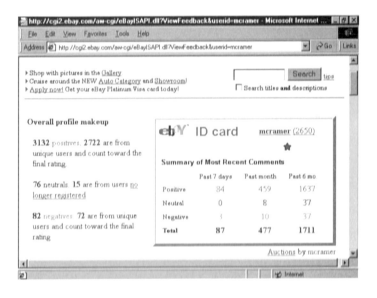

Before bidding at an auction, make sure to check out other buyers' comments about the seller.

- *Find out if the site carries auction insurance*—Auction sites recognize that sellers may commit fraud, and they want to make sure that people aren't so worried about getting ripped off that they don't bid. To combat that, many sites offer auction insurance where they will reimburse the buyer if the goods are never delivered after they're paid for, or if the goods aren't what they were promised to be. You don't need to pay for the insurance at these sites—you get the insurance for free when you bid.

- *Find out the precise details of auction insurance*—Different sites offer different kinds of insurance, and there's often a lot of fine print. eBay, for example, will reimburse you up to $200 if you've been scammed, although there's a $25 deductible, so you still have to pay $25. Amazon auctions, on the other hand, reimburse you up to $250 with no deductible. Both have fine print. So before you bid, check the insurance policies closely and make sure you understand them.

- *Check if you're buying from an individual or instead from a business*—On some auction sites, not just individuals sell items at auctions—so do businesses. If you buy from a business, you can usually pay with a credit card, and you may get a warranty as well. But you also want to make sure that the business is a reputable one. Look closely at the auction listing to see if you're buying from an individual or a business—that usually will be made clear in the fine print.

Icons may tell you if you're buying from a business

It's important to know whether you're buying from the site itself or from an individual. At first glance, it's not easy to tell where you're buying from at many sites. However, at some auction sites, such as Lycos auctions (*http://auctions.lycos.com/*), it's easy to tell when a business is doing the selling rather than an individual—there will be an icon identifying the seller as a business. The icon will be visible when you're browsing through the auction listings, not only when you visit a single listing. At Lycos and many other auctions, a gold star will indicate that the item is being sold by a business.

- *Use an escrow service for big-ticket items*—When you pay more than $200 or $250 at sites like eBay and Amazon, you're not covered by auction insurance. And not all sites offer such insurance. So how to cover yourself? Use an escrow service. When you use an escrow service, you pay the service instead of an individual. The service holds the money until the item is delivered, and it only pays the seller after you've received your item and say it's what was promised to you. For more information about escrow services, turn to Chapter 21, "Protecting Yourself Through Escrow Services."

Auction Sites Where You Buy from the Site Itself

On sites such as *www.surplusauction.com*, you buy directly from the site itself, not from individual buyers. When you buy from these kinds of sites, you usually get a warranty and generally can pay by credit card. They tend to have fewer kinds of things for sale than do sites where you buy from individuals, such as eBay. You need to know the following before buying and bidding.

- *Confirm that you're buying from a site, not from an individual*—Before bidding at any auction site, check to find out if you'll buy from the site itself or from individuals. It's not always easy to tell, but if there is no information about the seller at an auction page, that means you're buying from the site. Most sites in which you buy from them will also tell you that—check in the Help, Customer Service, or FAQ area to find out.

- *Get warranty information*—Often when you buy directly from a site, you'll get a warranty. Learn the terms of the warranty—particularly the duration of the warranty. Find out who provides the warranty, the site or the manufacturer of the goods you're buying. Find out if you have to do anything special to get a warranty, such as mailing in a card.

- *Check shipping costs*—Before buying from a site, see what you'll be charged in shipping. Unlike sites where you buy from individuals, you'll always pay shipping costs when you buy directly from the site. Costs should be displayed prominently. Make sure to check the shipping costs for every single item you bid on—the shipping costs may be different at each item for sale, even at the same site. The next figure shows the details of shipping costs and warranty information at the *www.surplusauction.com* site.

Here's how to find shipping costs and warranty information at the www.surplusauction.com site, where you buy directly from the site and not from other individuals.

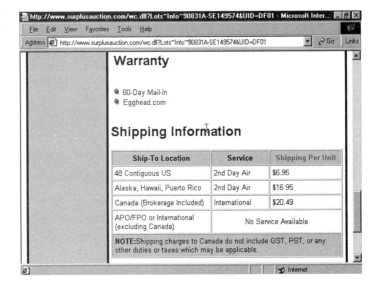

- *Find out if you have to pay taxes*—Because of the peculiarities of tax laws, if you buy an item directly from an auction site, you might have to pay taxes; if you buy from an individual, you won't have to. You'll only have to pay taxes if you live in certain states and buy from certain auction sites. For example, at the *www.surplusauction.com* site, if you buy and have goods shipped to the states of Washington or North Carolina, you'll have to pay sales tax. Check before buying.

- *Check if the items are refurbished or used*—Sometimes at auction sites where you buy directly from the site itself, some of the goods for sale may be used or refurbished. Check the auction listing carefully to see whether you're buying used or refurbished goods—and price your bids accordingly.

- *See how many of the items you're bidding on are up for sale*—Many times when you buy directly from auction sites, more than one of the item you're bidding on are up for sale— the site has often bought several lots of the item. Because of that, you can consider offering lower bids than if only one of the items were being sold. You'll often have to dig very carefully for the number of items that are being sold—it's often buried in fine print.

The World's Biggest Auction Site: eBay

eBay is a world unto itself. It's so much larger than other auction sites that many people don't bother to visit other sites—instead, they bid and sell only on eBay. There's good reason for this—as I write this, for example, there are over 2.5 million separate items being sold on eBay in over 1,600 different categories.

Because eBay is so large, comprehensive, and popular, I'll focus more on eBay than on other auction sites throughout this book. Most of the examples I'll give cover eBay, and many of the pictures I'll show you have to do with eBay as well. Most of the instructions, advice, and hints I offer about eBay, however, apply to other auction sites as well. For more information about eBay specifically, turn to Chapter 4, "eBay: The Biggest Auction Site in the Universe."

Specialized Auction Sites

The final type of auction sites you can visit are specialized auction sites. These are auction sites that specialize in a particular kind of goods, such as military memorabilia, coins, or stamps. If you're a serious collector, you'll want to visit these sites, whether or not you also visit general sites such as eBay.

These specialized auction sites may offer higher-priced goods than general auction sites because they specialize in collectibles. If you're buying a high-priced item, you should consider getting an appraiser or authenticator to check what you're considering buying, both to make sure the goods are the real thing and to give you a sense of what the item is really worth. Often, the sites have links to authentication and appraisal services. If you visit a site that doesn't have such a link and want an appraisal service, your

For More Information

There are hundreds of specialized auctions sites on the Internet, but how do you find them all? Most are little-known, off the beaten path, and have no marketing budgets. Well, there's a way to find them easily. Head to *www.internetauctionlist.com*, which bills itself as a "portal" to the auction world. It lists auctions by categories, such as coins, stamps, or boats. You'll be able to find links to many different specialized auctions from this site—it's the simplest way to find specialized auctions.

best bet is to head to eBay and find its links to appraisal services
and use one of those. The best way to find the links on eBay is to
click the Services button at the top of the site. You'll find links to
appraisers and authenticators there. For more information about
these services, turn to Chapter 22, "Using Appraisal Firms,
Verification Services, and Insurance."

Going, Going, Gone!

There are many different kinds of auction sites on the Internet,
and each has unique things you need to know before bidding and
buying. The following lists what you need to know before using
the sites:

- Before bidding at a Web site, know whether you'll be buying
  from the site itself or from individuals at the site. At most
  popular auction sites, such as eBay and the auction sites of
  Yahoo! and Amazon, you buy from individuals.

- Make sure to check out the seller when you buy from an individual at an auction site. Before bidding, look into the feedback section that lets people who have bought from the
  person before rate how reputable the seller is.

- Before you bid at an auction site where you buy from an
  individual, find out what kind of auction insurance the site
  has. If you're planning on buying a big-ticket item for over
  $200 or $250, consider using an escrow service. The escrow
  service takes your payment and then pays the buyer only
  when the item is shipped to you in good order.

- Before you bid at an auction site where you buy from the site
  itself, check the auction listing for warranty information,
  shipping costs, and whether you'll have to pay sales tax.

- At some sites where you buy directly from the auction site
  itself, the items are refurbished or used—and many may be
  up for sale at once. Check before you buy.

CHAPTER 3

Understanding Auction Basics

By now, you know what an online auction is and what kind of auction sites you can visit. But how do auctions work—how do you bid and buy?

In this chapter, you'll learn auction basics—how to bid and buy at all the kinds of auctions you'll find at the major auction sites.

Bidding and Buying at Basic Auctions

Before you can place your bids or sell at an auction, you'll need to know the basics of how each type of auction works. In this section, we'll cover the basic auction, which is the most common kind. In the rest of the chapter we'll cover other types of auctions. For more detailed information on bidding and buying, turn to Part 2, "Being a Savvy Buyer."

The Anatomy of a Bid

To bid at an auction, you first browse or search through a site to find an item you're interested in bidding on. For a more complete explanation of how to browse, searching and finding items, turn to Chapter 5, "How to Find What You Want to Buy."

Once you've found something you want to buy, you'll find a page that has all the information you'll need to place a bid. The next three figures break down what that page looks like on eBay. As you can see, someone is selling a set of old air mail stamps picturing the Graf Zeppelin.

What You'll Learn in This Chapter

▶ You'll find out how a basic auction is organized, what it looks like, and you'll learn how to bid at them.

▶ You'll learn how buyers and sellers determine how the item will be paid for, and how it will be shipped.

▶ You'll learn about all the different auction variations, including proxy auctions, Dutch auctions, restricted access auctions, private auctions and flash auctions.

Let the bidding begin: Here's the top part of the basic auction page where you'll bid on eBay. This part of the page displays all the vital bidding information.

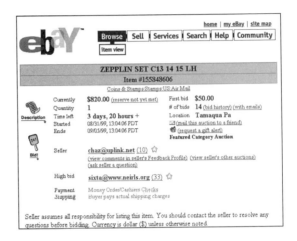

Here's the middle part of eBay's auction page. It's where you'll find the description of what's for sale.

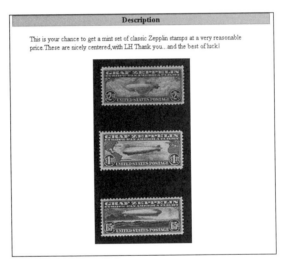

Before you make a bid on a page like this, you need to know how the page is organized. The eBay bidding page is divided into three parts:

- *The top part of the page*—Has all the vital information about the buyer, the current bidding price, the current high bidder, the number of bidders, when the auction begins and ends, payment and shipping options, and similar information. At some auctions, there's a minimum price that the seller is asking, below which he won't sell. If there's a minimum price, it will be listed here.

```
                              Bidding

           ZEPPLIN SET C13 14 15 LH (Item #155848606)

                   Current bid        $820.00
                   Bid increment      $10.00
                   Minimum bid        $830.00

  Registration required. eBay requires registration in order to bid. Find out how to become a
  registered user. It's fast and it's free!

  ┌─────────────────────────────────────────────────────────────────────┐
  │ To finalize your bid, you will need to submit your User ID and Password in the next step — │
  │ once you click on Review Bid.                                          │
  │                                                                       │
  │  ┌──────────────────────┐  Current minimum bid is 830.00   [ review bid ]  │
  │  Enter your maximum bid                                                │
  │  • Remember to type in numbers only and use a decimal point (.) when necessary. Don't include │
  │    a currency symbol ($) or thousand separator. For example: 1000000.00 │
  │                                                                       │
  │  Bid efficiently with Proxy Bidding — here's how it works:            │
  │   • Your maximum bid is kept secret, and it's not necessarily what you'll pay. eBay will bid on │
  │     your behalf (which is called proxy bidding) by steadily increasing your bid by small │
  │     increments until your maximum is reached.                         │
  │   • Why? Because it means you don't have to monitor the auction as it unfolds. You also don't │
  │     have to worry about being outbid at the very last minute unless someone bids over your │
  │     maximum dollar amount. Want more details? Check out an example of proxy bidding │
  │   • Choose your maximum carefully, though, as you won't be able to reduce it later │
  │                                                                       │
  │  Your bid is a contract                                               │
  │   • Only place a bid if you're serious about buying the item; if you're the winning bidder, you │
  │     will enter into a legally binding contract to purchase the item from the seller. │
  └─────────────────────────────────────────────────────────────────────┘
```

Here's the bottom of eBay's auction page, the place where you'll make your bid.

- *The description part of the page, located in the middle—* Here's where the seller describes what he's putting up for sale. In many instances, such as this one, a picture is included as well.

- *The bidding part of the page, located at the bottom—*This part of the page shows you the current high bid, tells you in what increments you can bid over the current high bid, and includes a place where you can make your bid.

Just a reminder, auctions at other sites will look different than this page, but in general, they'll all have the information presented here in some way.

The first thing to do when deciding to make a bid is to read the description carefully and examine the picture closely. After you do that, go to the information at the top of the page to find out when the bidding will close, look at the starting bid and the current bid, see the number of bidders, and to see the payment and shipping details and similar information. In our example, we see that the first bid was $50, that the current bid is $820, that there's three days and twenty hours left until the auction closes, that there's already been 14 bidders, that the buyer has to pay

Tip:

Before you bid on an item, you'll often want to see if there are other similar items up for bid. On eBay, that's easy to do. Just click the small link below the blue bar with the item number on it at the top of the description area. When you do that, you'll see a list of similar items up for auction. To do this on Amazon, click the If You Like This link on the right side of the screen.

shipping, and that the seller will accept only money orders or cashier's checks for payment.

After you've got all that information, you're ready to bid. Go to the bidding part of the page. In our example, the current high bid is $820, and the bidding increment is $10. That means that the next highest bid you can make is $830. To make your bid, type in the amount you want to bid. You'll get sent to another page to confirm your bid. Once you do, the high bid is yours. It will be listed as the high bid on the auction page. If no one outbids you before the auction ends in nearly four days, you've won, and the item is yours.

But let's say someone comes along and outbids you in three hours. Now he or she is the high bidder. You can come back later and bid higher. Bidding goes back and forth for the next several days until the auction closes. When it closes, whoever has the high bid is the winner and gets to buy the item.

So to sum up, here's how the bidding works at a basic auction:

- The seller lists the item for sale, determines for how long the auction will take, and may set a minimum bid that anyone who wants to buy must meet. A bidding increment is also determined, such as $1 or $10.

Bid at the last second to win

Many bidders win at auctions by bidding at the very last second to be the highest bidder. This technique, called sniping, is covered in Chapter 9, "Secret Techniques for Winning at Auctions."

- Buyers come to the auction listing, look at what's for sale, see what the current high bid is, and, if they're interested in bidding, outbid the current high bid.

- For the length of the auction, buyers continue to come by and bid against one another to win the auction.

- When the auction ends, the high bidder is declared the winner.

How You Pay (or Get Paid) at Auctions

Let's say that you've won the auction you've been bidding on— the rare Zeppelin air mail stamps are yours. It's time to pay and get the goods. What happens next?

The first thing that will happen after the auction closes is that you'll get an email notifying you that you're the winner and giving you the email address of the seller. The seller will get a similar email, giving him your email address. It's now up to you and the seller to complete the deal.

You and the seller will now communicate via email or by phone if you want. You'll decide on the method of payment and the shipping costs. You'll be told where to send your payment. The payment method or methods are usually specified on the auction page, so before you bid, you'll know in what way(s) you're required to pay. In our example of buying the Zeppelin stamps, the seller specified that payment had to be made by money order or cashier's check, so you'll pay in one of those two ways. Usually, buyers pay shipping costs—and again, in our Zeppelin example, that's what the seller specified. So you'll pay the shipping costs. Generally, you'll have a choice of shipping methods, and you can pay more if you want faster delivery.

After you exchange contact information and send the payment, the seller sends you the goods when he receives the check. It's that simple.

There are a lot of different ways you can pay or accept payment. Turn to Chapter 10, "Getting the Goods When You Win," and Part 4, "Completing the Deal," for more information. And there are a variety of ways to ensure that you don't get burned when buying or selling at an auction. Turn to Part 5, "Caveat Emptor."

How Proxy Bidding Works

The basic auction can prove to be time-consuming for bidders—you may have to constantly check the auction site, continually making a higher bid every time someone outbids you. Pretty soon, you'll lose interest because of all the effort it takes to win an auction.

A much easier way to bid is via what's called *proxy bidding*—a way of bidding that many major auctions sites use, such as eBay, Amazon, and many others. It's a way for you to, in essence, have a kind of robot do your bidding for you so you don't have to keep checking back at the auction. Here's how it works:

1. When you make a bid on an item, you bid for the maximum amount you're willing to pay for that item, regardless of what

You can often pay with a credit card when buy from the auction site

When you pay at a site in which you buy directly from the auction site, such as *www.firstauction. com*, you'll usually be able to pay via credit card rather than a money order, personal check, or cashier's check.

the current high bid is. Let's say, for example, that you're bidding on a porcelain figurine, and the current high bid is $20 with a bidding increment of $5. You've decided that you're willing to pay up to $75 for the figurine. So you bid $75.

2. You're now the high bidder—but at a price of $25, not $75. The $75 is a confidential price; no one but you knows that you're willing to pay $75 for the figurine. The price is $25, because it's the next highest bidding increment from $20. Your "proxy" at the auction site has bid $25 for you.

3. Another bidder comes by, and bids $30. Your proxy springs into action and ups the ante automatically to $35. You're still the high bidder.

4. Your proxy keeps bidding for you in this way, until the auction ends. If someone bids over $75, you don't win the auction. But if no one bids over $75, the item is yours—and you won't have to pay $75 unless the second low bidder is $70. Instead, you'll pay $5 more than the second high bidder. So, if the second high bidder bids $55, you'll win the auction for $60, not your $75 maximum bid.

By the way, you don't need to do anything special to do bidding by proxy at a site such as Amazon or eBay. And, as in any other kind of auction, if someone bids more than you, you can always go back and increase your bid until the auction closes.

How Reserve Auctions Work

There are times when someone puts something up for sale but is only willing to sell it at a certain price. In that case, a reserve auction is used.

In a reserve auction, the seller sets what's called a *reserve price*— a price underneath which he's not required to sell the item. Other than that, everything else about a reserve auction is the same as a regular auction.

The seller sets the reserve price, but that price isn't published. When you bid, you don't know the reserve price. You will know, however, if the high bid doesn't meet the reserve price—there'll be a note to that effect on the site. On eBay, that note is put right next to the listing for the high bid near the top of the auction page. Look back at the picture earlier in the chapter showing the Zeppelin stamp auction. You'll see near the top of the page that the current high bid is $820, and then in small print next to it, the note "reserve not yet met." That tells you that the auction is a reserve auction, and that the minimum price hasn't been met yet.

If the reserve price isn't met when the auction ends, the seller doesn't have to sell the item to the highest bidder. However, the seller *can* sell at below the reserve price if he chooses.

One confusing thing about reserve auctions is that there is also a minimum bidding price, which is published on the site, and the minimum bidding price is often below the reserve price. So why would anyone want to set a minimum bidding price that's less than the reserve price? This is often done because people selling using a reserve auction want to see what price they can get for an item without having to commit to selling it. Setting different reserve and minimum bids gives the seller a convenient way to test the waters, find out what he or she can get for an item, and then only sell it if he or she is happy with the price. That's because a seller can sell an item below the reserve price, if he chooses.

How Dutch Auctions Work

A popular kind of auction at many sites are Dutch auctions. Dutch auctions are commonly used when a seller has a number of the same items to sell—for example, someone who is selling 10 movie posters. In this kind of auction, all the winning bidders pay the identical price for the posters—the lowest successful bid. This means you can win an item at a Dutch auction at a lower price than you bid. However, at Dutch auctions, there's no proxy bidding, and no reserve price is set. Here's how it works in the example of someone selling 10 movie posters at a Dutch auction:

1. You see the movie posters at a Dutch auction and decide that you'd like to bid on one. It's worth $15 to you, so you bid $15.

2. Fourteen other people bid on the poster. Two people bid $20, seven bid $10, and five people bid $5.

3. The top ten bidders all get the poster for $10, because of the ten highest bidders, the lowest bid was $10. So even people who bid more than $10 get the posters at the $10 price. The people who bid $5 don't win the auction.

How Private Auctions Work

There are times when people want to bid on an item, but they don't want their identity known. Perhaps they're bidding on erotica or similar material. For whatever reason, they want their identity kept private.

If you're selling something at an auction site such as eBay, and are worried that bidders will be leery of having their identities known, you can set it up as a private auction. In a private auctions, the bidder's identities are never displayed. In every other way, the auction is the same—the bidding is the same, and the way payment works is the same.

How Restricted Access Auctions Work

eBay includes a special category of auctions, restricted access auctions, in which only adults are allowed to enter. Restricted access auctions are for adult material, such as erotica. Only adults are allowed to go to the restricted area. To go to a restricted access auction, you'll have to be registered on eBay, and they must have your credit card on file. That way, eBay can guarantee that you're at least 18 years of age.

You won't find restricted access auctions when you do a search—they're blocked from showing up when you do a search. The only way to get to one of these auctions is to click the Adult Only category. After do, you'll have to enter your password and username, and you'll only be granted access if eBay has your credit card. Once you're in the restricted area, the auctions work like any other auctions.

> **Restricted Access auctions don't have to be private auctions**
>
> It's easy to confuse restricted access auctions and private auctions, especially because adult material often is sold at both. However, restricted access auctions don't have to be private. So once you get into the restricted area, the auctions aren't necessarily private—that's up to the seller at each auction. There can be any type of auction in restricted areas, including Dutch auctions.
>
> Also, private auctions don't have to be set up as restricted access. A private auction can be set up in any area of eBay, not just in the restricted area.

How Flash Auctions Work

There's a kind of online auction you can participate in that works very much like real-life auctions. They're called *flash auctions*, and in them, you bid in real-time against other bidders, just as if you were at a real-life auction house. The only difference is that you're online, bidding live against others. The next figure shows a flash auction site.

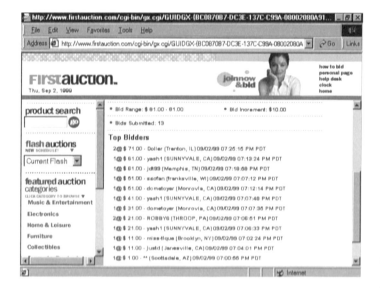

Here's a flash auction taking place at www. firstauction.com.

Flash auctions are usually held for short amounts of time, often an hour or less. You type in your bid, watch as others bid, and, if you want to outbid them, type in a higher bid. At the end of the auction, the highest bidder wins.

eBay doesn't offer flash auctions, but other sites, such as *www.firstauction.com*, do.

Be careful when bidding at flash auctions

Be careful that you don't get carried away by the moment when bidding at a flash auction. Keep in mind the most money you're willing to pay for the item, and stick to your guns— no matter how high the bidding gets.

Going, Going, Gone!

There are several different auction types you'll come across at sites such as eBay. The following are the most popular types, and what you need to know about each:

- *The basic auction*—In a basic auction, people bid against each other over a period of time, and, at the end, the seller and buyer make payment and shipping arrangements. The seller can set a minimum bidding price and determine the increments in which people can bid against one another. For example, the minimum bid can be $50, and the increment can be $5, in which case, the second bid after $50 will be $55.

- *Proxy bidding auction*—In proxy bidding, you set a maximum price that you're willing to pay for an item. However, you won't necessarily have to pay that amount if you win the auction. Your proxy bids automatically for you, by bidding the minimum increment over the current high bidder. For example, if you've set a maximum bid of $75, the bidding increment is $5, and someone bids $35, your proxy will automatically bid $40 for you. If the auction ends at that point, you'll get the item for $40, not $75.

- *Reserve auction*—In a reserve auction, the seller sets a minimum price, beneath which he doesn't have to sell the item. That price is known only to the seller. So, for example, if the reserve price is $75, and the high bid at an auction is $55, the seller doesn't have to sell. However, he still has the option of selling at a lower price than the reserve price, if he chooses.

- *Private auction*—At a private auction, the identity of the bidders are never displayed. The only person who knows the identity of the high bidder will be the seller. Other than that, all identities are kept private. These auctions are commonly used for selling things such as adult material.

- *Restricted access auction*—In a restricted access auction, only adults are allowed to view the auction and bid on it. Commonly, adult material is sold at restricted access auctions.

- *Flash auction*—A flash auction is very much like its traditional, real-world counterpart. In a flash auction, you bid against others live online. Flash auctions often last an hour or less.

CHAPTER 4

eBay: The Biggest Auction Site in the Universe

When you say the words "Internet auction" to someone, more often than not, the first site that will come to his or her mind is eBay. eBay is the largest auction site, by far, on the Internet, and, in essence, it was eBay that created the whole category of online auctions.

Because eBay is so popular, it has a huge number of items for sale. At some point, you'll want to visit there to see what all the fuss is about. As you'll see when you get there, it's a great auction site, not only because of the large number of items it has for sale, but for its services and organization as well.

In this chapter, you'll learn the basics of using eBay and get a guided tour of the site.

Getting Started with eBay

When you head to eBay, you'll see the front door—the main page of the site—which is shown in the following figure. From this page, you'll navigate to all of the site's many services, resources, and auctions listings.

The following are the most important parts of the page and what they do:

- *Categories*—A listing of the main categories of auctions you can bid on or sell at eBay. There are, in fact, more categories than just those you see here. To see them all, click the tiny More button at the bottom of the category list or click the Browse button at the top of the page.

What You'll Learn in This Chapter

▶ How to get started with eBay, and what you'll see on the main page.

▶ How you can register on eBay.

▶ The basics of how to buy and sell on eBay.

▶ How to use eBay's personal shopper.

▶ How My eBay can make it easier to master eBay.

▶ How Safe Harbor can make sure that you're safe when bidding and buying.

Note:

Touring eBay, you may notice mention of some auction activities that this book has not yet covered. Fear not—you're just meeting them here. You'll pick up the details in upcoming chapters.

*Here's eBay's main
page from which
you'll be able to
get to the auction
site's vast
resources, auction
listings, and ser-
vices.*

- *Sell Your Item*—Clicking here takes you to a form to fill out for selling your item at an auction.

- *Get News and Chat*—Clicking here takes you to an area on eBay where you can get information and updates about eBay and talk with other eBay users about anything you want.

- *New Users Click Here*—Clicking here takes you to the "new-bies" area of eBay—an extremely useful introduction to everything you need to know about eBay and auctions. In fact, even experienced users should consider going here because it's where you'll find comprehensive information about everything on the site.

- *Register*—This link takes you to the registration area. You'll have to register on eBay before you can sell and buy.

- *Featured*—Has a list of the featured items on eBay. Auctions are featured not because they're superior to other auctions, but because sellers paid an extra fee to have them in the fea-tured areas.

**You can buy on eBay
and do a good deed**

TV talk host Rosie
O'Donnell auctions
off items on eBay
autographed by her
and other celebrities.
Money from the auc-
tions is donated to
nonprofit organiza-
tions helping kids
throughout the
country.

Across the top of the main page, you'll find a set of buttons and links. These buttons and links are visible not only on the main page, but on many other eBay pages as well, so they're often accessible wherever you are. These buttons include the following:

- *Browse*—Takes you to a page which has a complete list of the categories and subcategories of items for sale on eBay.

- *Sell*—Like the Sell Your Item link, this takes you to a page where you can fill out a form to start an auction.

- *Services*—This links to a variety of eBay services, including escrow services, auction insurance, the feedback forum, ways to check your account status and change your account, and similar services.

- *Search*—Leads to a page that allows you to search through eBay for items in a variety of powerful, customized ways.

- *Help*—Leads to the eBay help area.

- *Community*—Leads to the discussion areas on eBay.

Across the very top of the page is yet another set of buttons that will be visible on many eBay pages as well, not just the main page. These buttons are

- *Home*—Clicking this takes you to the main eBay page. In this instance, you're already there, so clicking it isn't very useful.

- *My eBay*—Lets you customize eBay for the way that suits you. You can track all your bidding and selling, as well as your favorite categories, from one central place. I'll teach you how to use My eBay later in this chapter. It's one of the most useful features of eBay for regular users.

- *Site Map*—One of the great, underused features of the site. eBay is a vast, sprawling site, and it can be difficult to find the exact area you're looking for. The site map gives you a list of every area on the site, so you don't have to spend a great deal of time hunting for where you want to go.

How to Register on eBay

Before you can bid or sell on eBay, you'll have to first register with the site. It's easy and takes only a few minutes.

When you click the Register button, you'll go to a page that details the registration process and asks for the country in which you're located. After you choose your country and click to start the registration process, you'll go to the first registration page, shown in the following figure.

> **If you're worried about privacy, use the SSL link on the registration page**
>
> When you first start the registration process on eBay, you'll notice a link asking if you want to register using SSL. *SSL* stands for Secure Sockets Layer, and is a way of transmitting information over the Internet in an encrypted, secure manner so no one can snoop on the information you're sending.
>
> If you're worried about privacy, click that link—it'll make sure that the information you send will only be able to be read by eBay and no one else.

Here's the first form you'll fill out when registering on eBay.

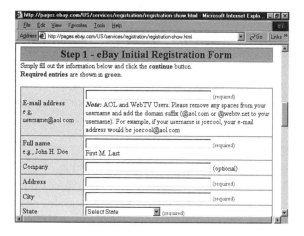

You have to register to participate in message boards

eBay's message boards are a great source of advice for buyers and sellers, but you can only participate if you first register with the site.

The form is a fairly standard one and primarily requires contact information. Some of the fields on it are green—those must be filled out for you to register. All the other fields are optional. These other fields ask personal and demographic information, such as your age, educational level, annual household income, and similar information. I prefer to leave them blank, but you should do whatever you're most comfortable doing.

Pay special attention to the email address you enter on the registration page. To complete your registration, eBay is going to send you a code via email. If you give out the wrong address, you won't be able to complete your registration.

After you complete this first registration page, eBay will send you an email message that has a confirmation code in it. Follow the link on the email back to the site and use this confirmation code to complete the registration. You'll also need your email address to complete the registration.

Before filling out the final part of the registration process, you'll be asked to read the eBay user agreement and to click a button verifying that you've read it. It's long, it's boring, and it's full of legalese, but you should still read it. It describes the dos and don'ts of the site and details your legal obligations.

On the final registration page, you'll be asked to choose a user ID, which in essence a nickname for you. It's the ID by which you'll be known on the site. You don't have to choose one—you can simply be known by your email address. You'll also be asked to create a password so that you can log in to the site. After you fill out this final page, you'll be an official eBay user and can start selling and bidding.

Be very careful when creating your password

When you create a password on eBay, you want to be very careful and make sure that no one can guess or steal it. Armed with your password, anyone can pose as you online, bidding and selling items and performing scams.

There are ways you can make sure that hackers or others can't guess your password. Don't use a password that is a word or that is the name of your spouse, children, or anything else associated with you. Use at least eight characters in your password; that makes it harder to guess than shorter passwords. And mix letters and numbers in your password—again, that makes it much harder to guess a password.

Buying and Selling on eBay

Buying and selling on eBay is no different from other major auction sites. Because you've gotten this far in the book, you know that the examples I've given throughout have always used eBay. So there's no need here to go into a great deal more detail about buying and selling on eBay. Just keep in mind the following whenever you buy and bid:

- The vast majority of auctions on eBay are done via proxy bidding, so keep that in mind when deciding when and how to bid on an item.

- If there's another kind of auction taking place, it will be clearly labeled.

- When you agree to sell or buy an item at a specific price, it's, in essence, a legal contract to buy or sell at that price—don't back out of it.

Using eBay's Personal Shopper

If you're a collector of a certain kinds of goods or want to know when certain kinds of items come up for sale for any reason, you'll find a great tool on eBay. It's called Personal Shopper, and you get to it by clicking the Site Map on the main page, and then selecting the Personal Shopper link.

The service automatically notifies you via email whenever an item comes up for auction on eBay that you might be interested in bidding on. When you first go to Personal Shopper, you'll see a page like the one shown next.

Fill out the form on eBay's Personal Shopper page and you'll get automatic email notifications whenever an item is up for sale that you might be interested in bidding on.

Type in a description of the item you're interested in being notified about, put in a price if you want, detail how often and for how long you want the notification to last, and you're done. You'll now automatically get email telling you when an item you might want to buy is up for sale. Note that you can only create three searches in your Personal Shopper.

Using My eBay

If you're an active eBay user, bidding and selling at many eBay auctions, it can be almost impossible to keep track of your activities. You'll have to remember all the auctions you're bidding on and auctions that you've created, keep track of your account balances, check out your feedback, browse through your favorite auction categories, and more. It can become practically a full-time job.

Luckily, eBay has a way that you can see all that in one place by visiting a single page—your customized My eBay page. It's the best way to manage your time on eBay, and it takes only a few minutes to set up.

To get there, click the My eBay link visible on most eBay pages. You'll see a page similar to the one shown in the following figure.

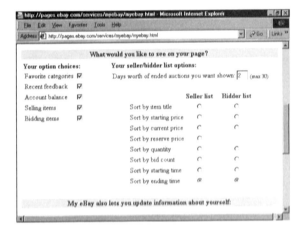

The best way to use eBay is through the My eBay feature. Here's the way you'll customize it.

From this page, you can choose what you want to display on your My eBay page. The following lists what you can show—or not show—on the page:

- *Favorite categories*—You can choose to display the categories on eBay that interest you most. On another page, you'll be able to choose up to four categories to display.

- *Recent feedback*—This will show you the most recent feedback left about you on eBay.

- *Account balance*—This displays your current eBay balance. When you get to your My eBay page, you'll be able to see

Create a personal Web page on eBay

You can create a personal Web page that lists your auctions and lets you promote yourself to others. To do it, click Create My Own eBay Home Page on your My eBay page.

your balance since your last invoice or the history of your entire account.

- *Selling items*—This displays the current items you're selling on eBay.

- *Bidding items*—This displays the items you're bidding on at eBay.

When it comes to displaying your auction listings on your My eBay page, you have a lot of options. You can sort them in a variety of ways:

- Item title

- Starting price

- Current price

- Reserve price

- Quantity (total number of items being sold at an auction)

- Bid count (number of bids on an item)

- Starting time (in Pacific Standard Time)

- Ending time (in Pacific Standard Time)

After you do all this, you'll have your own customized view of eBay. It's a good idea to go straight to you're my eBay page every time you visit the site. Shown next is part of a My eBay page.

Here's part of a customized My eBay page showing favorite categories.

Using eBay's Safe Harbor

eBay recognizes that doing business with people you've never met can be an unnerving experience. Knowing that, and that people want some protection against potential fraud online, the site has set up its Safe Harbor area. This area has a number of services designed to keep bidding and selling safe and secure. Get there by clicking the Services button on the main page, and then click the Safe Harbor button.

The following are the main services you'll find at Safe Harbor:

- *Feedback forum*—Here's where you can leave feedback about others or check out another eBay user's feedback.

- *Safe Harbor investigations*—This area of Safe Harbor details what kinds of auction abuses eBay will investigate and gives details on how to report abuses for potential investigations.

- *Escrow*—If you want to learn about how to use an escrow service, here's the place to go. eBay has a relationship with the i-Escrow escrow service, and you can get to that service from here.

- *Verified eBay user*—eBay is starting a program with the company Equifax Secure, Inc. to help guarantee that people are who they say they are on eBay to cut down fraud. For a $5 fee, people can apply to Equifax, which will take personal information and verify that the user is who he says he is. A special icon will appear next to all verified eBay users.

- *Insurance*—Here's where you'll get information about eBay's insurance program. You'll be covered for up to $200, with a $25 deductible. You're automatically covered; you don't need to apply.

- *Authentication & grading*—eBay offers advice to help you determine if a collectible is authentic and that its physical condition is properly graded. It includes links to authentication and grading services.

eBay's insurance won't cover every item and auction on the site

eBay's insurance policy won't cover every item for sale. Banned items aren't covered, and neither are auctions in which the seller or buyer has a total negative feedback.

Going, Going, Gone!

The eBay site is the biggest auction site in the world, and with good reason—it has a great set of features and services and has such a huge community of buyers and sellers that just about anything can be found for sale there. The following is a rundown on the most important things you should know about the site.

- Most of eBay's services and features are available directly from the main page. If you can't find a feature or service directly from the main page, click the Site Map, and you'll be able to find it there.

- Before you can bid or sell on eBay, you'll have to register. You'll fill out a form, receive an email with a confirmation code, and then return to the registration site to use that confirmation code to register.

- Almost all bidding on eBay is done via proxy bidding. In cases where there is a different type of bidding or auction—such as a Dutch auction—you'll be shown that on the auction page.

- eBay's Personal Shopper will automatically notify you when items come up for auction that you've indicated you're interested in bidding on.

- The My eBay area is an easy way to go to one place for all your eBay activity: tracking your bidding and selling, your favorite categories, and your account balances.

- eBay's Safe Harbor is where to go to make sure that bidding and buying are safe. You can get information about auction insurance, escrow services, fraud investigations, and more there.

PART 2

Being a Savvy Buyer

CHAPTER 5

How to Find What You Want to Buy

Every day, millions of items are up for bid at auction sites. On eBay alone, as I write this, there are nearly 2.7 million items up for sale in 1,628 categories.

That's both good news and bad news. It's good news because there's so much to buy. It's bad news because it means it can be hard to find the exact needle you want in the auction haystack.

In this chapter, you'll learn about all the ways you can find the exact item you're interested in buying. So, before you get lost trying to find your dream item to bid on, check out this chapter to learn how to get to that item as quickly as possible.

Starting Off with the Featured Items

When you visit any auction site looking to buy, the first things that will usually catch your eye are the featured auctions placed front and center on the page. If you look at the next figure of the front page of eBay, you'll see featured auctions right in the center of the page. Click any of the featured auctions and you'll be sent to an auction listing and can begin bidding. To see a complete list of featured auctions, click See All Featured.

If you're merely interested in browsing and don't have a specific thing you're looking to buy, you'll find the featured auctions an entertaining, eclectic mix. But you should be aware that there's nothing special about these auctions—the things being sold at them aren't any different from any other item sold on eBay. They're featured on the front page only because the seller has paid an extra $99.95 fee to eBay in addition to the normal auction fee.

What You'll Learn in This Chapter

▶ How to look through the featured items on auction sites.

▶ The best ways to browse through the categories and subcategories.

▶ How to refine the way you browse, so that you can view the items in different ways and find what you want faster.

▶ How to do basic searches.

▶ A variety of search tips so that you can narrow your searches only to specific items you're likely to be interested in bidding on.

▶ How to find and use the powerful search page on an auction site that offers a wide variety of highly customizable searches.

On eBay and
many sites, fea-
tured auctions are
front and center.
But the only rea-
son they're so visi-
ble is because the
seller has paid a
fee.

**Check out eBay's
grab-bag**

eBay's grab-bag area
is a great way to
find items for sale.
The grab-bag is
made up of thumb-
nail pictures of items
for sale. To get
there, click Grab Bag
at the top of the
screen.

Featured Items in eBay Categories

You'll find these featured items not only on eBay's front page.
They can also be found in each category and subcategory on eBay
as well. For example, if you click the Pottery & Glass category in
the left pane of eBay's front page, you'll go to a page that lists
pottery, glass, and porcelain auctions, and there will be featured
auctions in that category on that page. Then, from that page, if
you click Kitchen Glassware, for example, you'll find featured
items in the kitchen glassware category. Again, there's nothing
special about these auctions other than that the seller paid extra.
To get a featured item into the category or subcategory page costs
$14.95.

Browsing by Category

Checking out the featured items may be entertaining, but usually
when you come to an auction site, you have something more specific in mind to buy. A good place to start when you're looking
for something more specific is to browse by category.

Let's take an example. Say you're an antique doll collector. You
go to an auction site in search of antique dolls to buy. Here's how
to browse categories to find what you want quickly. In this
instance, we'll take a look at how to browse on eBay, but all

auction sites work pretty much the same when it comes to categories, with only slight variations.

All the categories in eBay are listed in the left side of the screen. You're looking for a doll, so click Dolls, Figures. You'll come to a page like the one shown in the next figure, which is the Dolls and Figures category page. The other figure shows what a category page looks like on *Amazon.com* auctions.

When you're browsing through an auction site like eBay, you'll come to category pages like this one, which also includes links to subcategories.

Here's how the category pages look on Amazon.com auctions.

The category page will have several featured auctions. Again, keep in mind there's nothing special about them apart from the fact that someone paid extra to have them featured.

As you can see from the picture, much of the category page is made up of a list of subcategories, such as General, Antique, Artist, Cloth, and similar subcategories. Click the subcategory that most closely describes what you're looking for. In this example, we've decided to look for antique dolls. So click the Antique link, and you'll go to the Antique doll subcategory, as you can see in the next figure.

A subcategory page on eBay— from here you'll browse through the auction listings themselves.

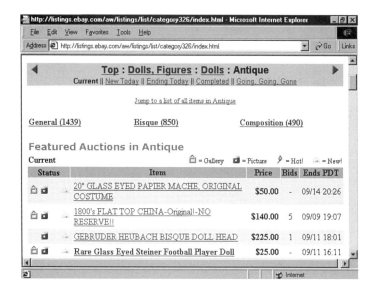

From this page, you can browse through the listings themselves. Just scroll down the page and read the descriptions; when there's an item for which you want more information, click it and you'll go directly to the auctions page where you can get more information and bid.

How to use the browsing icons

Icons placed next to auction descriptions on eBay will help you more easily browse through auctions to find what you want to buy. If you look at the previous picture from eBay, you'll notice a group of four icons below and to the right of the Featured Auctions in Antique title. The leftmost of these identifies an auction as being part of the Gallery.

The one next to it tells you there's a picture of the item on the auction page. The third one identifies a "hot" auction, which means an auction that has had more than 30 bids. And the fourth one tells you that the auction is a new one. Look for these icons to the left of an auction listing when you browse.

On some subcategory pages, like the one shown earlier for Antique Dolls, there are even *more* subcategories—General, Bisque, and Composition. Click any of them and you'll get a list of all the auctions in that further subcategory.

Refining the Browse Listings

When you browse through categories like this, the list of auctions you'll see is often quite substantial—you'll often have 10 or more screens of listings to go through. This can make it difficult to find the exact auctions you're interested in. On eBay, and on many other auction sites, you'll be able to refine the way you browse through listings.

Look back at the subcategory page I showed earlier in the chapter. You'll see four links at the top of the page that you can click to refine your browse. The following is a list of what they mean on eBay. Again, other sites will have similar links, so check those sites for what those links will do.

- *New Today*—Lists all the auctions in that subcategory that have been created today. This is especially useful for you if you frequently check into eBay and only want to see newer auctions you haven't seen before.

- *Ending Today*—Lists all the auctions in that subcategory that will end today. This is useful for those people who prefer to bid very late in the auction process. (For more information about bidding strategies, turn to Chapter 9, "Secret Techniques for Winning at Auctions.")

- *Completed*—Lists all the recent auctions in the subcategory that have already been finished. At first, this may seem an odd thing to list—why would you want to see auctions that have already been completed? The answer is that it's a great way to help you decide what to bid on current auctions—

you'll be able to see the current going rates for items on which you may bid.

- *Going, Going, Gone*—Lists all the auctions in the subcategory that are going to end within the next five hours. This is useful for those who like to bid as late as possible in the bidding process.

Doing a Basic Search

If you're looking for a specific item to buy quickly, there's a faster way to find it than to browse through the categories. You should use the auction site's search feature instead.

On almost any auction site—including eBay—the search feature will be available on every page. To use it, just enter the word or words that describe the item you're searching for in the search box at the top of the page, in the same way that you'd use a search engine such as Yahoo! or Lycos.

For example, say you're a big Elvis fan, and you're looking to buy an original 45 rpm record of his single *Jailhouse Rock*. Browsing through the categories isn't the way to find such a specific item. Do a search instead.

Your first instinct might be to simply search Elvis. Big mistake, especially if you're on eBay. When I did it just now, it led to a listing of 4,855 items. So you want to do a much narrower search.

Type in **Elvis** and **45**, and your search is still too broad; I just did it and got 296 auctions. But if you type in **Elvis jailhouse rock 45**, you'll hit paydirt—that leads to seven auctions, all of which are selling 45s of *Jailhouse Rock*.

The moral of this story: Make your search as focused as you possibly can by using as many words as possible to describe the item for which you're looking. Just make sure not to make the search *too* narrow, otherwise, you'll overlook some items you might have wanted to bid on.

On eBay, when you do a basic search, you're searching through only the titles of the auctions, not through the longer descriptions of the items. If you want to search through the descriptions of the items, check the box on the Search Results page that says Search Titles and Descriptions.

Search Tips for Getting the Best Results

There are a lot of ways auction sites such as eBay let you focus and narrow your search. The following are some top tips to make sure you spend the least time searching for what you want and make sure you get exactly what you want when you search. These tips all work on eBay, and most will work on other auction sites as well.

- *Delete or add the letter "s" to your search*—Let's say you want to buy old 45 rpm records. Search on both **45** and **45s** to get the most complete search results.

- *Use quotation marks to search for exact phrases*—Say you're searching for a copy of the classic movie *The Wizard of Oz*. If you type in all those words by themselves, you may get a lot of auctions that contain any of the words. If you put quotation marks around the name of the movie, you'll only get auctions that contain the precise phrase.

- *You don't have to use the word "and"*—On eBay, if you want to search for an auction that contains both of two or more words, such as poster and Godzilla, just type in **poster Godzilla**. It'll find every auction with the words Godzilla and poster in it. You don't need to type in the word "and." Doing a search this way will tend to narrow your search.

- *Use a comma and no space after it if you want to use the word "or"*—Say you wanted to find every auction with either the words Godzilla *or* poster in it. Type in **Godzilla,poster**. Note that there's no space between the first and second words. Doing a search like this will broaden your search.

- *Use the – sign to narrow your searching*—Say you want to find posters, but don't want any posters of Godzilla. You would use the – sign to narrow your search (**poster - Godzilla**). That would find auctions of posters, but not if any of the posters was of Godzilla.

- *Sort the items by ending date, bid price, or search ranking*—When you do a search, it sorts the results by the starting date of each auction. That's not necessarily the best way to find

For More Information:

For the complete rundown on search tips and secrets and the exact phrasing and syntax to use on eBay, head to *pages.ebay.com/help /buyerguide/search. html.*

what you want—you might be looking for an item at a certain price or whose auction will end on a certain date. At the
top of each page on eBay, there's a drop-down box that lets
you sort your search results according to the ending date of
the auction, the bidding price, and how likely the auction is
to match your search terms. Use that box to re-sort your
searches. The following figure shows that box being used.

A good way to find what you're looking for is to re-sort your search results, such as viewing the results by the bidding price. Here's how to re-sort your items when doing a search on eBay.

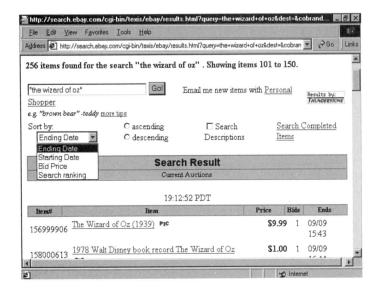

Using an Auction Site's Advanced Page

Many auction sites offer highly targeted search pages that make it
easy to do exceptionally advanced searches. They'll let you find
auctions based on things such as the bidding range, the sellers
identity, the location of the seller, and more. To get to this page on
eBay, click the Search button at the top of almost any page.
Check other auction sites to see where their advanced search
pages are located.

The following are the different sections on eBay's advanced
search page and how you can use them to do better searches:

- *By the title listing*—As in a normal search, you can search by
  title listing. But on the advanced search page, you can also
  put in a price range, the country where the item is located,

and you can search the title of the auction as well as the auction description.

- *By the item number*—Every item on eBay (as well as on many other auction sites) is identified by a specific number. If you recall the item number, you can type it in. When you get a search result, you'll go straight to the auction itself, not a Search Results page.

- *By the identity of the seller*—If you know the User ID or email address of a seller, you can search for all the items he or she has listed. This is especially useful if there's a particular seller who often has the kinds of items you're interested in buying.

- *By the identity of the bidder*—If you know the User ID or email address of a bidder, you can search for all the items he or she has listed. This is useful for sellers who want to check out a bidder who's bidding on an item of theirs. I've also found it useful as a reminder to myself to check everything on which I'm bidding. I just search on my ID, and I see all the auctions in which I'm involved.

- *By completed auctions*—When you're trying to decide what you should bid on an item, a good way to find out a reasonable price is to see what similar items have sold for. You can search by completed auctions on this page to see the final selling prices on items.

For More Information: If you want to search for items at many auction sites simultaneously, head to *www.biddersedge.com* or *www.auctionwatch.com*. Both sites search multiple auction sites, so you can bid at any of them—not just one.

Going, Going, Gone!

Many auction sites are huge, rambling places, filled with up to several million items. If you know what to do, though, it's easy to find the exact item you'd want. Here's how to do it:

- If you don't have a specific item in mind you're looking to buy when you get to an auction site, check the featured items. However, keep in mind that the reason they're featured on eBay (and often on other auction sites as well) is that the seller has paid extra to give them more visibility—there's nothing else special about the featured auctions.

- Browsing by category and subcategory is a good way to find broad categories of items you're interested in buying, such as antique dolls or beaded jewelry.

- If you want to find a specific item, you're better off using the auction site's search feature. Be as specific as possible when doing a search by using the words most relevant to the item you're looking to buy. If you do too broad a search, there will be too many items to search through.

- Every auction site has its own rules for searching. Find out how to narrow searches at each site by searching for two or more words in the title of an auction, such as Elvis 45. There are also special rules for how to use words and special characters on each site. Look for help on how to do it at whatever auction site you're on. On eBay, the page that will get you help is *pages.ebay.com/help/buyerguide/search.html*.

- Most auction sites have a special search page that lets you narrow searches by doing things such as searching on a bidding range, the identity of the seller or buyer, and similar features. Look for it when you want to focus your search.

CHAPTER 6

Checking Out a Seller Before Bidding

After you've found an item you're interested in buying, the next step is to check out the person who's doing the selling. You should check out a seller before bidding so that you don't get burned by someone who takes your money and either doesn't deliver the goods or doesn't deliver them as promised. You should also check out the seller to get more information about how much money you should bid on the item.

In this chapter, you'll learn how to check out a seller before making a bid. You'll see how to use the feedback features of auction sites to find out how reputable the seller is, and you'll also learn how to check out the seller's other auctions and how to send email to the seller before you bid, as a way of gauging how responsive he is. We won't cover how you can give feedback about sellers in this chapter. To learn how to do that, turn to Chapter 10, "Getting the Goods When You Win."

Keep in mind that if you're a seller at an auction, you can also check out a buyer, by following the same advice outlined in this chapter. Turn to Chapter 17, "Making Contact with the High Bidder," for more information on how you, as a seller, can check out a bidder.

Why You Need to Check Out the Seller

When you buy from someone via an auction site, you're buying it from them sight unseen. So it's important that you check out a seller before you bid. You want to make sure that the person is reputable and will deliver the goods in good order and in the time to which you've agreed. Probably the best way to make sure that

What You'll Learn in This Chapter

► Get a quick rundown on how reputable buyers think the seller is.

► Find how many more people think the seller has done a good job than people think he has done a bad job.

► Find the seller feedback page to read every comment made by buyers about the seller.

► Check out a seller's other auctions before making a bid.

► Get a feel for how responsive the seller is to potential buyers and why this is important.

you never get burned on an auction site is to check out the seller before you bid.

Auction sites provide different ways to check out sellers. Most of them, at a minimum, allow buyers to make comments about sellers from whom they've bought. And some sites, such as Amazon, allow buyers to rate the sellers—in Amazon's, on a one-to-five star rating system.

But no matter how the sites let you check out sellers, the following is what you should be looking for when you look into a seller:

- *Has the seller sold many items previously?*—If you're dealing with a new seller or one who has sold very few items, there's very little track record to go on, so be careful when bidding.

- *Has the seller received almost all positive feedback?*—If a seller has received mixed reviews from buyers, you'll probably want to bid elsewhere. On the other hand, if the seller has only one bad review and many good ones, that may indicate that the person giving the review was the problem, not the seller.

- *Were the goods what was promised, and delivered on time and in good order?*—Some of the most frequent complaints about sellers is that the goods weren't what was promised were not packaged well and arrived damaged, or were delivered late. Read through the comments to see how well the sellers handle these circumstances.

- *Was the seller responsive via email or other methods?*—As a buyer, you'll may have questions about the item for sale or its delivery. You want to make sure that the seller is responsive to questions from buyers.

Step One: How to Get Basic Feedback About a Seller

The first step you should take when checking out a seller is to get basic feedback about them. For most purposes, you won't need to delve into a great deal of detail about the seller's feedback from buyers. If you're buying a reasonably priced item, $50 or less, you really only want to know whether the seller has received positive feedback as a whole from other buyers. You don't need to read individual reviews.

Sites such as Amazon, eBay, and others make it easy to get quick feedback about a seller at a glance. To get the feedback, just go to an auction page. On eBay and most other sites, that page will have a way to get quick feedback about the seller. On eBay, there will be a small colored star icon next to the name of the seller and a number next to the star. The color of the star tells you the range of positive comments that have been posted about the buyer at a glance. The number tells you the precise number of positive comments posted about the buyer, minus the number of negative comments. For example, if a buyer gets 195 positive comments and three negative comments, his rating will be 192. The following figure shows an example of the star and rating on eBay.

eBay takes negative comments seriously. In fact, if someone ends up with a –4 or worse total rating, all the privileges to buy and sell on eBay are taken away from them. Someone can get a negative rating if there are more negative than positive comments about them.

Here's what the different colored stars mean on eBay. Again, keep in mind that each auction site uses different kinds of rating systems, so check each site for their rating system.

- A yellow star means a net rating of from 10 to 99 more positive comments than negative comments.

- A turquoise star means a net rating of from 100 to 499 more positive comments than negative comments.

Tip:

Not all auction sites require that everyone participate in the feedback program. On Amazon, for example, the seller has the option not to participate.

Note:

Sometimes when you're looking at an auction on eBay and look for the star rating next to the seller, you'll also see a little icon of the word Me. Click that icon and you'll go to what eBay calls the About Me page. It's a page that any eBay user can create that gives information about someone such as their background, interests, items they're interested in buying and selling, and almost anything else the person wants to put there. Also on the page will be other people's feedback about that person. The feedback can't be chosen by the person himself; instead, it's put on that page by eBay.

Look for the star and number next to it on eBay to get basic feedback about the seller of an item...

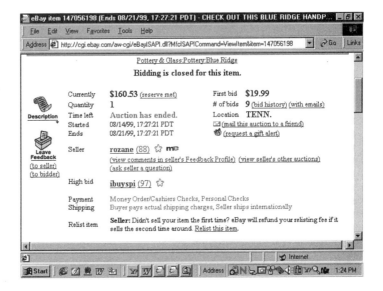

...and on Amazon, you also look for a star and a number.

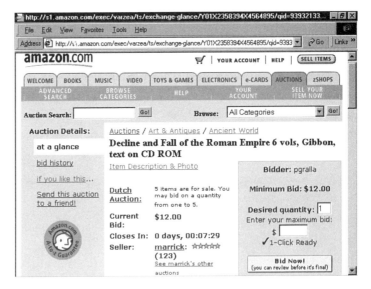

- A purple star means a net rating of from 500 to 999 more positive comments than negative comments.

- A red star means a net rating of from 1000 to 9,999 more positive comments than negative comments.

- A shooting star means a net rating of 10,000 or higher more positive comments than negative comments.

Step Two: Getting Detailed Feedback Information About a Seller

After you've gotten basic feedback, you might want to get more detailed feedback information about the seller. If you're bidding on a big-ticket item, or if you just want to be extra careful about who you buy an item from, you can get more detailed feedback about a seller. On eBay, for example, you'll be able to read every comment everyone has about a seller. And you'll also be able to view a detailed summary of the person's feedback.

To do this on eBay, click the link underneath the seller's name that reads View Comments in Seller's Feedback Profile. When you do that, you'll go to a page that details all the feedback about a seller. At the top of the page is a summary of all the feedback about the person for the last seven days, the last month, the last six months, and for the entire length of time the person has been on eBay. You can see a summary in the following figure.

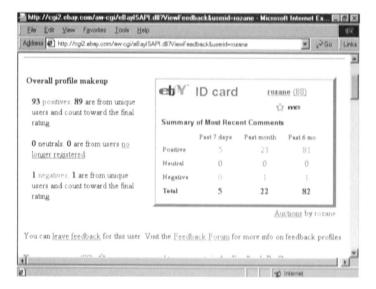

Here's a detailed summary of a seller's feedback on eBay.

Scroll down the page, and you'll see all the specific comments made by customers who have bought from the seller. If there's more than one page of comments, you'll be able to see more comments by clicking links at the bottom of the page.

You can get to the seller feedback page without having to go to the auction page first

There's a way to look at a seller's feedback page without having to go to one of their auction pages on eBay. Instead, click the Search button at the top of any eBay page, and then click Find Members from the page that appears. You'll be led to a page that lets you find a seller's feedback page by searching for it. You'll need to know the seller's user ID, which is either their email address or a nickname that he or she has chosen.

Helpful in these comments is that the identity of those who have made comments is made public, so you can send email to those people for follow-up information. You can also see *their* ratings, which will help you decide whether their ratings were fair or not. Pictured next is an example of comments made about a seller on eBay.

If you want the most information about a seller on eBay, scroll down the feedback page so you can see every individual comment made about them.

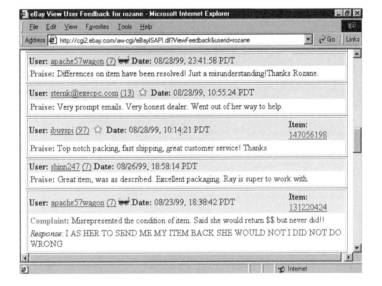

What the Shades Icon Means on eBay

On eBay, sometimes you'll see a small icon of sunglasses—what eBay calls "shades"—next to a seller's name. That icon means that the person has changed his user ID within the last 30 days. After that person has used the new user ID for 30 days, the shades icon disappears.

While there are perfectly legitimate reasons why someone might have changed a user ID, if you see a shades icon next to a seller, you should take extra care to examine that person's feedback. It's possible that the person has changed user IDs because he or she has received too much negative feedback and wanted to use a new ID that didn't have negative feedback associated with it.

There's a simple way to see all the person's feedback, not only for their current ID but for previous IDs as well. Click the shades icon. That will lead to a list of all the person's previous IDs. You can then check out the feedback on each of those IDs.

Step Three: Check Out a Seller's Other Auctions

Investigating a seller means more than just checking out his or her feedback page. You should also see what other items the seller has up for bid. Why bother? There are many reasons. The following are the most important:

- *It will show you whether the seller specializes in the item you're bidding on*—If the seller has an eclectic variety of items up for sale and no particular specialty, you'll know that he's probably not an expert in the particular item you're bidding on. This means that you shouldn't necessarily take his word about the authenticity or importance of certain items.

- *It may lead you to other items that you want to bid on*— Many sellers specialize in certain kinds of items. If that's the case, they may have other items similar to the one you're bidding on.

- *You may find the same or similar items at a lower price*— The seller may well have the identical or similar items he's auctioning. If so, you may be able to find the same or similar item at a lower price.

- *It will help you determine how much to bid on your current auction*—If the seller has similar items up for bid at other auctions, checking those prices will help you decide what to bid on the current auction.

Pretty much any auction site you visit will let you easily check out a seller's other auctions, so check each site to see how to do it. On eBay, click View Seller's Other Auctions, on the auction page, and you'll get a complete list of his or her current auctions.

Make sure to count on more than just the feedback listings

No matter someone's feedback rating, the basic consumer rule holds on auction sites: If something sounds too good to be true, it probably *is*, so don't bid.

Step Four: Send Email to the Seller

The final step you should take to check out a seller is to send him or her an email. It's easy to do this at any auction site. On eBay, click Ask Seller a Question on the auction page and you'll be able to send him or her an email.

When you send an email, ask for more information about the item for sale and any other questions you can think of. You want to see how responsive the seller is to you, and how trustworthy and knowledgeable he or she seems. If he or she doesn't respond quickly and helpfully to you when you're considering bidding on an item, you should expect him or her to be even *less* helpful and responsive after receiving your money if you've won the item.

Going, Going, Gone!

Before making a bid, you should always check out the bidder:

- Before placing a bid, find out how many other items the seller has sold, see whether he's received positive feedback, and find out if buyers have been satisfied with the quality of the items he's sold and his responsiveness.

- Most auction sites let you get quick, basic information about a seller by their use of a star rating system. The system can be a one-to-five star rating system (such as Amazon's), or a colored star rating system (such as eBay's). You'll usually see the stars or similar rating system on the auction bidding page next to the name of the seller.

- To check out a seller more completely, review the user comments about him or her on a feedback page. The page will usually have listings of every comment made by others who have won bids on the seller's auctions. It's especially important to do this if you've bidding on big-ticket items.

- It's a good idea to check out a seller's other auctions. This will help you determine whether the seller specializes in one or more kinds of items and will help you judge whether he's an expert in the items he has for sale. It may also lead you to identical or similar items for sale and help you determine what you should bid on the item you're interested in buying.

- Send email to the seller to see how well he or she answers your questions and if they are answered quickly and completely. If a seller doesn't get back to you promptly and completely before you've bid, he or she probably won't be responsive to you after you've bought the item.

CHAPTER 7

Buyer's Checklist: What to Do Before Making a Bid

The key to getting the best deal when bidding at an auction is to first do your homework. When you get caught up in auction fever, it's easy to forget that the real point of bidding at an auction isn't to win—it's to get the goods you want at the best price possible. Overpaying for an item just so you can beat out the competition may be good for your ego, but it's bad for your pocketbook.

In this chapter, you'll learn how you can check out any item before making a bid, so that you'll make the best bid possible and never pay more than necessary. You'll find out how to uncover the true cost of an item and how to determine the ideal bidding price. You'll learn how to make sure you don't get hit by any hidden costs after you buy, such as shipping or sales tax. And you'll find out when you can expect to get a warranty and return policy.

By the way, you should always also check out the seller before bidding. It's so important, in fact, that I've devoted an entire chapter to it. The previous chapter, "Checking Out a Seller Before Bidding," told you everything you need to know about checking out a seller before making your bid.

Step One: Search the Internet for the True Cost of an Item

To teach you what to do before making a bid, let's take a real-life example. Let's say you're an aficionado of old Pez dispensers. On eBay, you've found an Indian chief dispenser up for auction, and it's the perfect item to round out your collection. Let's step through what you need to do before bidding.

What You'll Learn in This Chapter

▸ Find out an item's real price by using Internet search sites and online shopping sites.

▸ Check out other auctions for similar items, and look for the items' selling prices.

▸ Examine the item's bidding history to see if there was a bidding war.

▸ Find out the shipping costs of an item and factor that into your bidding.

▸ Look for warranty and return information.

▸ Wrap it all up and get ready to bid.

Start off by using the Internet to find the true cost of an item before you bid. Sellers use lots of tricks to make a product sound appealing (and I'll teach you those tricks throughout Part 3, "Auction Marketing 101."). Before bidding, do your research and find out what the item is selling for elsewhere online. It'll only take a few minutes, and you'll be surprised at how much money a simple check can save you.

I'll show you two ways to use the Internet to search for what an item should sell for:

- *Internet search engines*—These Web sites will find all kinds of information about an item for you—everything from pricing information to ways you can verify an item's authenticity.

- *Online shopping sites*—These Web sites are best for finding out the true selling price of new goods. You won't use them for collectibles, such as Pez dispensers, but you will use them for items such as new Palm computers.

Use Web Search Engines for Getting Pricing and Other Information

Web search engines will find pricing information for you and comprehensive information on what's being sold. In many cases, they'll lead you to experts or appraisers who can give you advice on how to gauge the proper buying price for just about anything. Armed with the proper information about pricing and the goods being sold, you'll be able to decide whether to bid, and, if you decide to bid, you'll be able to get the best price possible.

To use them, go to one of the popular search sites, such as *www.lycos.com*, type in a word or words that describe what you're looking for, and you'll receive a comprehensive list of related Internet sites.

How to fine-tune your Web searching

When you're using a search engine to find specific information about something you want to buy, you can quickly become overwhelmed with the number of sites recommended to you—sometimes hundreds or more. To get a more targeted list of relevant sites, fine-tune your searching. For example, instead of searching for the single word Pez, search for the phrase Pez dispenser. To do that, use quotation marks around the phrase when typing it ("Pez dispenser"). That way, you'll search for the entire phrase, and you won't search for the word Pez and the word dispenser.

You can also often use the words AND and OR when searching. When you use the word AND, it will only find sites that have both words in them—it narrows your search. For example, if you type in *Pez AND Indian*, it will find only sites that have both words in them. When you use the word OR, it broadens the search. For example, if you type in *Pez OR Indian*, it will find all sites that have *either* of the words in them. Because of this, be careful when using the word OR.

You can also combine using quotation marks with AND. To fine-tune a search, for example, type *"Pez dispenser" AND Indian*.

By the way, each search site is different, and not all may follow these kinds of searching conventions. Check the specific search site you're using for details.

So to find information about the Indian chief Pez dispenser, go to *www.lycos.com*, and type in the word *Pez*. You'll find a list of dozens of sites. Read the descriptions of the sites and click any that sound like they have information that will help you set your bid.

In our example, I found several, including *www.pezheads.org*, a site that includes an online price guide for old, collectible dispensers. I found out that the average price for an Indian chief dispenser on eBay is $137, and the average price is $175 elsewhere on the Internet.

By using a search engine, which took about 10 minutes, we were able to find the going price on eBay for the dispenser we're interested in buying.

Tip:
Other search engines to use beside Lycos are *www.altavista.com*, *www.excite.com*, *www.google.com*, *www.go.com*, and *www.yahoo.com*.

Find the Lowest Price at Online Shopping Sites

After you've checked out search engines, head to online shopping sites to find pricing information. They're particularly helpful for getting pricing information for new items for sale. For old collectibles, such as a Pez dispenser, these sites won't do much good—they really only help if you're buying something new.

At auction sites such as eBay, if you want to buy a new item, the seller will usually tout the "retail price" of the item and hype how much you can save if you buy at auction prices instead of through a retail store. But is the price they quote the true selling price?

To find out, go to one of the popular selling sites, such as *www.buy.com*. Type in the name of the product whose price you want and up will pop the selling price and other information about the product. You'll now have the true selling price of the product—not the "retail price" hyped by the auction seller.

New Indian chief Pez dispensers are no longer being sold, so you won't find information about one at an online shopping site. But here's a real-life example: Shortly after they were released, new Palm IIIx digital organizers were a fairly hot item at auction sites. The suggested retail for them was $369, which was prominently hyped by many auction sellers at eBay and beyond. I found the IIIx selling for up to $275 at eBay, and there were sellers asking for at least $310 for them at several auction sites, including Yahoo auctions.

I checked the popular *www.buy.com* online shopping site and found the Palm IIIx selling for $244—far less that it was being auctioned for at various auction sites. So I knew the highest price I should pay for one at auction was $244.

To find the true selling price, you can either check out a general shopping site, such as *www.buy.com*, or a site that specializes in the goods being sold, such as *www.fogdog.com* for sporting goods.

When looking for the true cost of an item, don't confine yourself to the Web. Check out real-life retail stores as well. They may have even lower prices than Web stores.

Step 2: Find Similar Items on Auction Sites and Compare

After you've checked out the Web for pricing and other information about the goods you want to buy, take the next step and get pricing information even closer at hand—prices provided by the auction sites themselves.

It's easy to do that at eBay. (Other auction sites do it differently, so check those sites.) First search for an auction as you would normally—in our example, by typing in the word *Pez*. That will show you all the current auctions still open that are selling Pez items. But those auctions are still open and bidding is still going

For More Information:
Before bidding, look for prices at *www.comparenet. com* and *www. mysimon.com*, which compare prices at many online shopping sites. Also be sure to check out *www.buy.com* and specialty buying sites. For a comprehensive list of online shopping sites, check *The Complete Idiot's Guide to Online Shopping*.

on, so we don't know what the final selling price will be. The only way to get a true selling price is to look through *completed* auctions because they list the final selling price.

To find final prices at completed auctions on eBay, after you've searched for an item, click the Search Completed Items link on the upper-right of the page—you can see it in the following figure. When you do that, you'll see a list of auctions that have already closed, and you'll see the final selling price of each of the items.

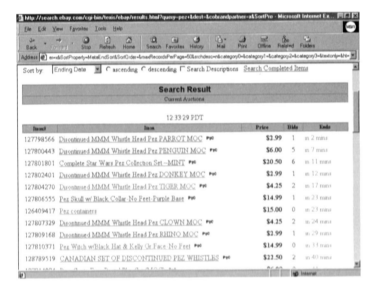

Click Search Completed Items to look for completed auctions and selling prices on eBay.

Doing that, I found that an Indian chief Pez dispenser sold for $117.50 the last time it sold on eBay. Now we know to keep bids in that range.

Next, check other auction sites for pricing as well, so you can get a truer picture of the going rate for what you're bidding on. You may find the same goods for sale at lower prices.

Instead of checking each site individually, go to one of the several auction *shopping robots* or *AuctionBots*—Web sites that will show you auctions taking place at several dozen auction sites. The best one is BiddersEdge at *www.biddersedge.com*. Head there and search for your item, just as you would at any auction site. You'll see a list of auctions selling the item, and you'll see them from well over a dozen different auction sites. From this one site, you'll be able to get an overview of pricing at auctions across the entire Internet. BidFind at *www.bidfind.com* performs a similar service, although it's not as nearly comprehensive.

After checking out these sites, I found that, for the moment, no other Indian chief Pez dispensers are being sold at other auctions. So for now, at least, eBay is the only game in town.

Step 3: Check Out an Item's Bidding History

An item's selling price won't tell you the whole story about what you should bid. Before making a bid, you should also check an item's bidding history. A bidding history shows you every bid made by every person on an item in an auction. You should check the bidding history because sometimes the price at an auction is the result of a bidding war among two or more people who, for egotistical or other reasons, are willing to pay what may be an exorbitant price for something. You shouldn't base your own bidding on the result of a single, oddball bidding war.

You'll only be able to see bidding histories at completed auctions. To do that on eBay, click Bid History at a completed auction and you'll see each bid made by every person at the auction. The following figure shows you the bidding history on an Indian chief Pez dispenser at eBay.

Here's what you'll see when you check out an item's bidding history on eBay.

When checking a bidding history, you're looking to see how fast and furious the action was—frequent bidding by two or more people in a short amount of time is a sign of a bidding war. Also look to see whether there are two or more bidders who seem to be bidding more than the rest of the pack. When you come across signs like these, keep in mind that the final winning price may be a high-priced anomaly, so don't base your own bids on it.

Check out auction re-listings before you bid

There are times when a seller will pull an item from an auction; he'll take it out of the bidding. Usually, this happens when his minimum asking price—usually called the reserve price—isn't met. Very often, the seller will wait some time and then put the item up for bid again, at the same minimum price or possibly at a lower price. This is called re-listing.

Knowing whether an item has been re-listed will help you determine what price you should bid. If an item has been re-listed at least once, it means the seller is having a hard time selling it, so consider lowballing when you bid. And if it's been re-listed several times, that's an even bigger indication you should lowball.

To check whether an item has been re-listed, first check the current auction details. Included in those details will be the name of the seller. Click the seller's name, so you can see the complete list of all the items he's put up for bid. Look at all the items. If you see the same item being put up for bid more than once, and the sales were never completed, you'll be able to see which items have been re-listed.

In this case, as you can see, there's been no bidding war. There have been only seven bids, and no back-and-forth jockeying. So that means the $117.50 price paid for the item is one you can rely on—no egos or bidding wars were involved.

Step 4: Check Out the Shipping Costs

Should you be the high bidder, the price you'll bid at an auction is only a portion of the price you'll actually pay for an item. You'll also have to pay shipping costs.

Shipping costs vary for each auction because the seller sets his own shipping costs. Shipping costs vary widely. They can be as little as $2 or $3, but for larger items, you can pay $30 or more, especially if the item is going to be insured, or if you want it delivered via some kind of express delivery service.

Tip:
When checking
shipping costs, make
sure that the costs
look reasonable. A
seller can try to
gouge sellers by
charging inflated
shipping costs.

It's easy to check out shipping costs at eBay. When you look at an auction, you'll see a line that says Shipping, and it has information about shipping costs—or at least it should. Sometimes, you'll have to check the description of the item to find out shipping costs. (Check other auction sites to see how they list shipping costs.) If the cost isn't listed or is vague, send an email to the seller asking for the costs. If you don't get an adequate response, don't bid.

In some instances, you'll also be charged sales tax. The laws on sales tax and the Internet are quite murky, but generally speaking, no sales tax will be charged. But if you're buying an item from an established business and you happen to live in the same state where that business has a main office, you may have to pay sales tax. The seller will be responsible for informing you whether you'll need to pay the sales tax.

In our case of a Pez dispenser, because it's a small item, we see that the shipping is minimal—only $3.20. And it's being sold by an individual, so there's no sales tax. These costs aren't going to add much to the over $100 we'd be willing to bid on the Pez dispenser.

In other cases, though, shipping costs and sales tax can add up. For example, I found a laptop computer at eBay being offered for $1000. The deal sounded good, but then I added in the shipping costs of $30 and the sales tax of 8.25 percent for California residents, and came up with a true cost of $1,120.50 for someone living in California—more than 12 percent over what the price at first seemed.

Step 5: Find Out the Return Policy and Warranty

When you buy something at an auction, you usually won't find a return policy or warranty. You assume that what you buy will arrive in good shape, and that it'll be precisely what's described online. Any disagreements will be negotiated between you and the individual seller, and individual sellers don't offer warranties.

But at times when you buy at eBay or other auction sites, you'll be buying from an established business and you may get a warranty. At sites such as OnSale at *www.onsale.com*, for example, you'll buy directly from the site itself and will usually get a warranty. On most auction sites, including eBay, Yahoo's auction site, Amazon's auction site and others, businesses as well as individuals are selling items. These items can be new, especially if they're computer products.

Before buying a new product from a business at an auction site, check out the warranty and return policy. Ideally, you should get at least a 30-day, no-questions-asked return policy. And if it's a new item, it should carry the full warranty for the item.

You'll find warranty information in the item description on eBay. Again, if that information isn't included in the auction description, send an email to the seller. If you don't get an adequate answer, don't bid.

See if the seller has a Web site where he sells goods

Always look for links to Web sites in auction listings to see if the seller has a Web site where he sells goods. You may be able to find a better price and more goods there.

Step 6: Wrap It All Up and Bid

So let's see what we found out by doing research before making a bid.

- We found out that the average selling price on eBay for our Indian chief Pez dispenser is $137, and elsewhere on the Internet the average price is $175. So we have a general idea of what we should bid on the item. And we know that eBay prices tend to be better than on other auction sites, so it's a good place to shop for this dispenser.

- We haven't found any shopping sites selling the Pez dispenser—no great surprise because it's a discontinued item.

- We've checked other auction sites and found that, at the moment, there are no other Indian chief Pez dispensers for sale.

- We found out that the last time a similar Pez dispenser sold on eBay, it sold for $117.50. And we know no bidding wars were involved, so it's a real price.

- We know the shipping costs ($3.20) and saw that there's no warranty on the item.

Based on all this, it's easy to decide on what to bid. Start bidding at under $117.50. If you're overbid and have to bid against someone else, you know you can go to $137 and still only be paying the average eBay price for the item. And you know that elsewhere on the Internet, the item has been sold for an average of $175—so if this is something you really want, you can gamble and bid all the way up to that price.

Going, Going, Gone!

Before bidding on any item, you should use the Internet and auction sites to find out the true cost of the item to help you determine your best bid. You should also check shipping costs, warranties, and return policies. The following should be your plan of attack:

- Go to Internet search sites, such as *www.yahoo.com* or *www.lycos.com*, to find out information about the goods up for sale.

- Head to Internet shopping sites, such *www.buy.com*, to find out the current lowest selling prices for the item online.

- Check auction sites to see at what price similar or identical items have recently sold.

- Examine items' bidding histories to help you get a better handle on what you should bid.

- Read the fine print in auction listings for information about shipping costs, sales tax, return policies, and warranties.

CHAPTER 8

Bidding Basics: How to Place Your Bids

By now you've found the item you want to buy, you've checked out the seller, and you've gone through the buyer's checklist of what to do before making your bid—so you've decided on the price. Now it's time to place your bid. In this chapter, I'll teach you how to actually make your bid at an auction. Note that this chapter covers the mechanics of bidding, while the next chapter, Chapter 9, "Secret Techniques for Winning at Auctions," covers bidding strategies.

Step One: Check Out the Item Details Page

You've found the item you're interested in buying, you've made sure that the bidder is a reputable one, and you've researched the item you're interested in buying, so you know what price you're willing to pay for it. So you're ready to bid.

When it's time to bid, first go to the page that has all the details about the item you're buying—it's the page that will let you do your actual bidding. From there, you'll get all the information about the item being auctioned, the terms of the auction, and you'll be able to place your bid.

Let's take an example. We'll use eBay in it, but just about every auction site will work similarly. Say that you're collector of baseball cards, and you interested in buying the rookie cards of Mark McGwire and Sammy Sosa. You've found an auction that you're interested in, and you've done all your homework. It's time to bid.

Go to the auction page, which on eBay is commonly known as the Item Detail page. As I explained in Chapter 3, "Understanding Auction Basics," there are three parts to this page on eBay:

- *The top part of the page*—Has all the vital information about the buyer, the current bidding price, the current high bidder, the number of bidders, when the auction begins and ends, payment and shipping options, and similar information.

What You'll Learn in This Chapter

▶ How to get all the relevant information about what's for sale from the auction page, such as the bidding price and increment, the name of the seller, the number of bids, and the length of the auction.

▶ How to place your bid, after first double-checking and reviewing it to make sure it's the right price.

▶ How to follow up your initial bid checking the auction page regularly to see if you're still the high bidder

▶ How to contact the seller via email to arrange for payment and shipping if you're the high bidder.

• *The item description*—Where the seller describes what he's putting up for sale.

• *The bidding part of the page, located at the bottom*—This is where you'll make your bid. It also shows the current high bid and tells you in what increments you can bid over the current high bid.

The following figures show you the three parts of the Item Detail page. Again, keep in mind that auctions at other sites will look different than this page, but they'll still have similar information to what you see here.

You'll get all the vital information about an auction—bidding price, when the auction ends, and similar information—on the top of an Item Detail page on eBay.

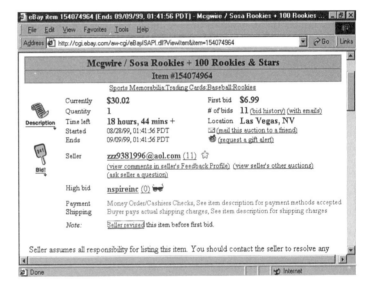

First things, first. Read the description and look at the pictures, if any. That's the most complete description you'll find of the item you're bidding on.

After that, go to the top of the page, which has the vital information about the auction and the seller. You should look at every piece of information in this section of the page before bidding. The following lists the important information you'll find there, and what you should know and do before making your bid:

• *The title bar*—Centered in the middle of the page, tells you what the item is that's up for bid. In our example, it tells us that there are 100 baseball cards of stars and rookies up for sale, including those of Mark McGwire and Sammy Sosa.

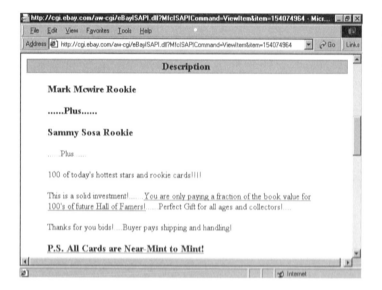

In the middle of an Item Detail page on eBay, you'll find the description of item up for sale.

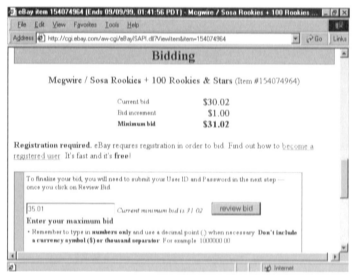

At the bottom of an Item Detail page on eBay, you get bidding information and do your actual bidding.

- *The item number*—Gives you the unique number that identifies this auction. Copy it down somewhere and keep it safe—with so many items up for bid on eBay, it sometimes can be hard to find an auction once you've visited it. With the item

number, you'll always be able to get back to it by using the
search page.

- *The category listing*—Tells you the item's category and subcategory. This is useful if you'd like to look for similar items.
Just click the link and you'll be sent to the subcategory with
auctions similar to the one you're currently on. In our example, you'd see a list of other rookie baseball cards up for sale
if you click the link.

- *Currently*—Shows you the current high bid—in our example,
$30.02. When you're browsing and searching through the
site, you may notice that sometimes the current price you see
on a browser or search page is lower than the current price
you see on this page. That's because the browse and search
pages aren't updated as frequently as this page. This page has
the true current high bid.

- *Quantity*—Tells you the number of items up for sale. The
more items up for sale, the greater your odds of winning the
auction at a lower price—keep that in mind when bidding. In
this case, there's only one item up for sale.

- *Time left*—Tells you how many days, hours, and minutes are
left until the auction ends. Jot down this information so that
you'll know when to check back to see if you've been outbid
or to place a bid if you haven't already done so. In our example, we have 18 hours and 44 minutes before the auction
closes.

- *Started*—Tells you when the auction began.

- *Ends*—Tells you when the auction will end. Again, jot down
this information so you know when to come back and bid.

- *Seller*—Tells you who is selling the item. Chapter 6,
"Checking out a Seller Before Bidding," tells you how to use
this information and what it means.

- *High bid*—Tells you who the current high bidder is. You can
get the same information about the high bidder as you can
about the seller. For example, you can read the feedback
comments about the bidder by clicking the number in

**You can get vital
information about
the auction from
your browser's title
bar**

On eBay, the title
bar at the top of
your browser win-
dows has the ending
date and time of the
auction, the item
number, and the
item that's up for
bid.

parentheses. In our example, you can see the name of the high bidder, that he has yet to receive feedback, and that he's changed his ID within the last 30 days. Because of that, there's a chance that even if he wins the auction, he may not end up paying for the item, and so the second high bidder will get the goods. You may want to gamble and not make the highest bid, hoping the high bidder never follows through on the purchase.

- *Payment*—Tells you how you can pay for an item. In our example, you'll be able to pay by money order and cashier's check. That's a very common way to pay at auction sites, including eBay.

- *Shipping*—Tells you who pays for shipping, and, in some cases, what the amount will be. In almost all cases, the buyer pays for shipping. Shipping prices aren't always detailed in the listing. Before bidding on an auction with no shipping costs listed, you should send an email to the seller asking for the shipping costs.

- *Note*—Gives you any other miscellaneous information about the listing. In our example, you can see that the seller revised his auction listing before someone placed the first bid. It could have been for something as simple as a typographical error or something larger, such as that no one placed a bid, so he lowered his initial asking price.

- *First bid*—Tells you what the initial bid on the item was. Often, but not always, the seller specifies an opening bid. The initial price, the current price, and how long the auction has been open will give you clues about how much to bid. If the auction has been going on for some time, and there's little difference between the initial and current bids, it may well mean that there's not a great demand for the item. In our example, the initial price was $6.99, the current price is $30.02, and the auction has been open for more than 11 days. That probably indicates the cards won't be sold for a great deal of money.

You can ask the seller a direct question on Yahoo! auctions

If you have a question about an item for sale on Yahoo! auctions, click the Ask Seller a Question link at the bottom of the page. You'll be able to fill out a form to ask your question.

- *# of bids*—Tells you how many bids have been placed so far. Again, fewer bids means an item that's not in great demand. In our example, 11 bids have been placed—about one a day. To see the bidding history—who placed each bid and when—click the Bid History link. If you also want to see email addresses, click the With Emails link. Note that you won't be able to see the prices that people have bid while the auction is still live—you can only see the prices after the auction has closed. Even so, the bidding history has clues for you on what to bid. If there haven't been bids recently, you stand a better chance of winning the auction because interest in the item has died down.

> **Use gift alerts and mailing auction information to friends**
>
> Participating in auctions need not be a solitary experience. Two little icons and links let you notify friends and family about auctions that might interest them—or tell them that you've bought something for them and that a gift is on the way. Click the little icon of the letter or the Mail This Auction to a Friend link next to it, and you'll be able to send an email to anyone notifying them about an auction that might interested them. You'll be identified as the sender of the email.
>
> If you click the little gift icon or the Request a Gift A, you can send an email to someone notifying them that you've bought them a gift at an auction on eBay. You can only send a gift alert if the auction has closed and you're the high bidder, and you'll have to send it within 30 days of the auction close.

- *Location*—Tells you where the seller lives. This is especially important if the buyer will be paying for shipping and it's a large item—meaning that shipping costs may be substantial. If the seller lives near you, you can drive over to his or her house or place of business to examine the item or pick it up if you're the high bidder. In our example, the seller lives in Las Vegas, land of the high rollers.

Step Two: Place Your Bid

After you've gone through all the details about the auction, it's time to place your bid. We'll go over how to bid on eBay, but the way you bid at other auction sites is quite similar; just check each individual site for details.

When you want to bid, scroll to the bottom of the page or click the Bid icon. Whichever you do, you'll go to the bidding part of the page, as shown in the third figure in this chapter.

Bidding is exceptionally easy. Just enter your bid in the bidding box and click the Review Bid button. Right above the box, you'll see the current high bid, the bidding increment, and your minimum bidding price. Enter that price or higher, depending on what you're willing to pay. Remember, eBay's auctions are proxy auctions, which means that if you win the auction, you won't necessarily have to pay your highest bidding price. Instead, you'll pay the minimum bid that lets you win the auction—the second highest bidder's bid plus the minimum bid increment. While many popular auction sites such as eBay, Amazon, and others use proxy bidding, not all do, so check each individual auction for rules. For more information about proxy auctions and other auction variations, turn to Chapter 3.

By the way, you haven't formally bid after you enter your bidding price. You'll still have a chance to back out of the auction when you review your bid. So don't be afraid to click the Review Bid button.

When you click the Review Bid button, you'll go to a page where you enter your username and password. You'll also see your bid there, so that you can make sure it's correct. The following figures show this page on eBay and on Yahoo! auctions.

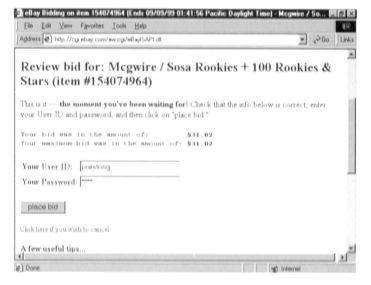

Here's the page on eBay where you review your bid. Make sure it's what you want, and then place your bid.

Here's the page where you'll review your bid on Yahoo! auctions.

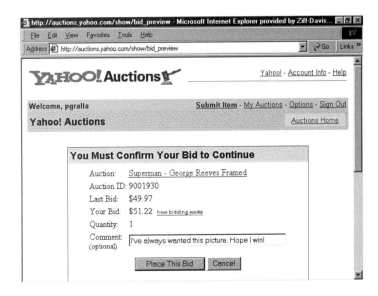

What to do if you've forgotten your User ID or password

When you register at eBay, you'll have to create a User ID and a password. Whenever you want to bid or create an auction on the site, you'll have to log in using your ID and password. But what if you've forgotten your User ID or password? You can use the email address you used at registration instead of a User ID—eBay will recognize it. If you've forgotten your password, click the Password link on the Review Bid page, and you'll receive an email from eBay giving you instructions on how to get a usable password of your choosing.

To place your bid after you've entered your username and password, click Place Bid. If you decide you don't want to bid or want to change your bid, either use your browser's back button or click the Click Here If You Wish to Cancel Link (underneath the Place Bid button).

There's both art and science to bidding, and I'll cover those in Chapter 9. But the most basic rule of thumb for bidding is this: Bid the maximum amount you're willing to pay for an item, and then don't go over it by a dollar. Keep in mind that you'll be paying shipping costs, so factor in that cost when making your bid.

After you place your bid, you'll be sent to a confirmation page, shown in the next figure. As you can see, it tells you the amount you've bid on the item, whether you're the high bidder, or whether you've been outbid. In our example, we didn't bid high enough—someone else bid higher.

If you wanted to bid again, you would click the Bid Again link and continue raising your bid until you were the high bidder. If the price was too high, you could go and look for a new item to bid on.

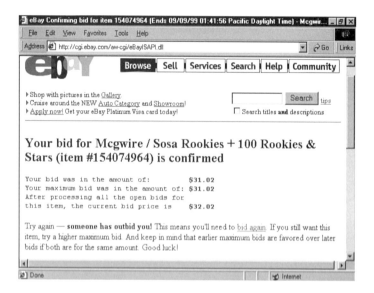

Close but no cigar: This page confirms our bid on eBay. But someone has outbid us, so we'll either have to bid again or let someone else win the auction.

Step Three: Follow Up on Your Bidding

If you're the high bidder on eBay and many other auction sites, you'll receive a confirmation email with all the relevant details—your bid price, the item you're bidding on, and how much longer the auction will last. Every day after that, you'll get a daily email update, confirming that you're the high bidder and restating the relevant information.

Often though, you're going to be outbid by someone. When that happens, you'll get an email from the auction site telling you that you've been outbid, listing the current high bid, and including a link to go back and outbid the current high bidder if you'd like. Repeat the bidding process as often as you want if you want to become the high bidder.

If you want to be absolutely sure that you win a particular auction, don't rely on being told via email that you've been outbid. Instead, regularly check back on the auction yourself to see if you're still the high bidder. If you're not the high bidder and still want to win the auction, raise your bid.

You won't always be notified when you've been outbid before the auction closes

Most of the time, you'll be notified via email that you've been outbid on an item in plenty of time to go back and submit a higher bid. But if you're outbid in the final moments before an auction closes, there won't be time to notify you via email that you've been outbid. If you really want to win, don't rely on email and watch an auction closely.

Step Four: Close the Deal

Let's say the big moment finally comes. You've done your bidding, you've followed the auction, it closes, and you're the high bidder. Now what?

On most sites, you'll be notified via email that you're the high bidder, and the seller will be notified as well. At this point, it's up to you and the seller to make arrangements for payment and shipping. Then, after you've paid for the item and it's been shipped to you, fill out a feedback form about the buyer. This lets other eBay bidders know your experiences with the seller.

For more information on closing the deal as a buyer, turn to Chapter 10, "Getting the Goods When You Win." For help making sure you never get burned as a buyer, turn to Part 5, "Caveat Emptor."

Going, Going, Gone!

When you've found the item you want to buy and checked out the bidder, it's time to make your bid. The following is a summary of what to do when bidding on an item:

- Gather all the relevant information about the auction before bidding. Among other details, look for the current price and bidding increment, the length and ending date of the auction, the number of bids, payment and shipping information, and how many items are up for bid.

- Read the description of the items for sale closely and carefully examine any photographs. It's the only chance you'll get to examine the items before placing your bid.

- After you enter the your bid, you'll usually be given a chance to review your bid before it's final. Double-check that the information is correct before placing your final bid.

- If you're the high bidder, you'll be notified on the bid confirmation page, and will usually be sent a follow-up email as well. If you're not the high bidder, you usually won't be sent an email—instead, you'll be notified on the bid confirmation page.

- You'll generally be sent an email notifying you when you're outbid. However, don't rely on always being sent an email as a way of tracking your auctions. Instead, visit the auction page regularly to track the bidding yourself.

- If you've won the auction, you and the seller will be notified via email. It's then up to the two of you to arrange payment and shipping.

CHAPTER 9

Secret Techniques for Winning at Auctions

As you learned in the last chapter, it's relatively easy to bid at auction sites. But simply making a bid isn't the point at an auction, you want to be able to get the item you want and at the lowest possible price.

In this chapter, I'll teach you secret techniques you can use to win at auctions. You'll learn how to decide on the proper price for a bid, when to make the bid, how you can win auctions by as little as a single penny, and how to auction *snipe*—a technique for bidding at the last possible moment before an auction closes.

How To Determine Your Best Bidding Price

Here's the most basic bidding question of all: How much should you bid for an item?

The quick-and-easy answer is that you should bid the maximum amount you're comfortable paying, and you shouldn't budge a dollar over that price. Whatever an item is worth to you is the amount that you should bid. Because most auction sites, such as eBay and Amazon, use proxy bidding, you often won't have to pay that maximum amount should you win.

Of course, nothing in life—and certainly nothing in auctioning—is really that easy. You want to make sure that you don't overpay for an item, and you want to be able to get the item at the lowest possible price.

For more details on how to research the true cost of any item up for bid at an auction site, turn back to Chapter 7, "Buyer's Checklist: What to Do Before Making a Bid." The following is a short rundown on how to find out the true cost of an item and set your bid price:

What You'll Learn in This Chapter

▶ How to research the true selling cost of an item.

▶ How to use a simple technique so you can outbid others by pennies.

▶ When the best time is to bid on an auction—at the beginning, middle, or the end.

▶ How you can get the best deals at Dutch auctions.

▶ How to become the best auction sniper possible to get the best price in the last moments before an auction closes.

▶ What software you can use to help you become a power bidder.

- Use Web search engines to find as much information about the item up for sale, including any current or used selling prices, if available.

- Use online shopping sites to find out the retail price of the item, if available.

- Find similar items for sale on several auction sites and determine the general going rate for the item.

After you do all this, you'll know how much you want to bid, so you're ready to buy.

How You Can Outbid Others by Pennies

Doing your homework ahead of time will help you decide what price you should pay for an item. But the odds are that others are doing their homework as well, and they'll probably come up with bidding prices similar to yours.

There's a simple way you can win auctions when a number of bidders will all be bidding nearly the same price. You can use odd bidding amounts in increments of pennies, and become the highest bidder at an auction. So, while everyone else will be bidding $50, you'll bid $50.01, and you'll be the highest bidder because you outbid others by a penny.

Let's take an example and see how it works. Say that you're bidding on a leaf blower for your lawn. You've done your research and you think a good, fair price for it would be $70. Your first instinct would be to bid $70.

Don't let your emotions get the best of you when bidding

A word to the wise: Don't get carried away with needing to win, and let your emotions get the best of you when bidding. Focus on the worth of the item you're bidding on, not on whether you get the winning bid.

But if other people bid $70, the first person who put in that $70 bid will win, and perhaps it won't be you. So, instead of bidding $70, bid $70.01. The auction closes with several $70 bids, but you bid a penny more ($70.01), so the leaf blower is yours. Kiss your old rake goodbye.

Keep in mind that you don't have to always bid only one cent above a rounded amount. Any odd number of cents will do, such as $70.07 or $70.23.

The Best Time for Making Your Bid

Next to setting your bid, one of the most important decisions you'll make about bidding is when to place your bids. There are a lot of different points of view about the best time. There are those who believe that the best technique is to bid as early as possible, others who favor waiting until the last minute, and still others who think you'll do best if you continually check the site and re-bid throughout the life of the auction.

There are reasons why you'll take each of these approaches. At one auction you might want to bid early, while at another you may wait until the end. The following lists what you need to know about the timing of bidding and when you should use each strategy:

- Bid early if there is something up at the auction site that frequently is sold, there's a well-established going price, and you want to pre-emptively win the auction. Let's take an example. Say that you're a fan of Godzilla action figures. You've been on the auction sites, you know that the selling price on them fluctuates between $10 and $15, and you know that they regularly show up. You really want one of these beasts. So the next time one comes up, immediately bid $15. Because that's the current top going price, other bidders won't bother to try to outbid you. Instead, they'll wait around until another comes up for sale and try to get a lowball price on it.

- Bid early if you don't like to have to keep checking back on the auction site to see the current selling price. On eBay and some other auction sites, when you're the high bidder, you'll get a daily email notifying you that you're still the high bidder or that you've been outbid. At whatever point you get outbid, you can go back to the site and re-bid.

- Bid low when you bid early if you want to keep coming back to the auction page to see how the bidding is going, upping your bid each time you return. You'll do this if you want to feel out other bidders to get a sense of how high they'll bid before you make your high bid. I find this the trickiest way to bid and tend not to use it that much.

Before you place a
bid, walk away from
your computer, come
back and then bid

Before making a bid,
ask yourself whether
you really want the
item and can afford
it. Then walk away
from your computer.
When you answer
the questions and
return, you'll have a
clearer head about
bidding.

- Bid late if you're the type who wants to get an item at the absolute lowest price, can deal with pressure situations, and enjoy the thrill of the chase. When you bid at the end, you're most likely to get the item at the lowest possible price because all the other bids have been placed—except by others who enjoy late bidding. A variation of this is called *sniping*, which is covered in the "Learning How to Snipe" section later in this chapter.

How to Get the Best Deals at Dutch Auctions

The bidding tips we've learned about in this chapter so far pertain to normal auctions, particularly to the proxy bidding that's done at many popular auction sites. But when you bid at Dutch auctions, they don't apply at all—there's a different technique you should use.

First, a refresher about how Dutch auctions work. In a Dutch auction, a seller has multiple copies of an item he's selling, such as 10 Beanie Baby Brittania Bears. The highest ten bidders all win, but they'll all pay the lowest qualifying bid. For example, if of the highest ten bidders, one person bid $90, two bid $87, two bid $85, four bid $83, and one person bid $80, those ten people would all get the bear for $80, the lowest qualifying bid.

The key to bidding at Dutch auctions is really very simple: You want to be one of the highest bidders, but you don't want to bump up the lowest qualifying price causing you and everyone else to pay more than you necessary. To see this in practice, let's take the example of a Dutch auction of ten Brittania Bears. You come into the auction and, as I stated in the preceding paragraph, of the highest ten bidders, one person bid $90, two bid $87, two bid $85, four bid $83 and one person bid $80. You want to make sure that you're one of the highest ten bidders, and you want to make sure that you're protected and won't get bumped out of being one of those ten.

You have to bid more than the lowest bidder—if you don't, you won't get one of the bears. At first glance, you might think the best thing to do is bid $81. After all, if you do that, you'll be one of the qualifiers, but you'll only raise the price everyone pays for the bear to $81. Here's the problem, though: If you do that, it's easy for someone to come by and knock you out of the running. If someone bids $82, you'll be out of luck.

The best technique is to bid just below the highest current price. In this example, you'd bid $89, and everyone would pay $83, the lowest qualifying bid. By bidding just below the current high price, it becomes difficult to knock you out of the running—there are a lot of lower bidders who act as buffers between you and getting locked out of the auction.

Learning How to Snipe

Many bidders looking for the best deal at auction sites use a technique called sniping. It's time-consuming and can be nerve-wracking, and you often lose out to other snipers. But still, it's an excellent way to get the best deal possible at an auction.

The idea of sniping is quite simple. You want to make your winning bid at the last possible moment before the auction closes, so that no other bidders have a chance to see your high bid and respond to it (outbid you).

Becoming a good sniper takes a good deal of practice. The following steps show the general way to do it:

1. When you find an item you're interested in buying, and you plan on sniping to get it, write down the auction number—so you can easily get back to it—and note the date and time the auction ends.

2. About a half-hour before the auction closes, go to the auction page. See what the current high bid is. Every few minutes, reload the page by clicking your browser's Refresh button, pressing Control+R, or however else your browser reloads. Watch what happens. Are the bids changing? If they are, it means that there are probably other snipers present, so you know that you'll have to be fast if you want to snipe and get the goods.

3. Within about five minutes of the auction's close, reload your page more frequently to see how hot and heavy the sniping action is, if there is any.

4. Open up a second browser window. You'll be using one browser window to check the bidding status and the other window to do the actual bidding.

When sniping, don't have any programs open other than your browser

When you're sniping, close all programs except your browser. That way, your computer won't respond sluggishly or be prone to crash, and you'll be more likely to win the auction.

5. As the clock ticks down, continually refresh one browser window to check on the status of the auction.

6. Note the highest current bidder in that browser window as close as possible to the auction closing. In the other browser window, type in a higher bidding price—the highest price you're willing to pay. Don't formally enter the bid yet; have it ready, but wait until the last possible second to confirm your bid.

7. At the last moment possible, place your bid. Now hold your breath and refresh the browser window as the auction closes to see if you've won.

As you'll find out when you snipe, sometimes you'll be the only sniper, and it'll be easy to win your auction. At other times, however, you'll be beaten by another sniper. Take a look at the following figure. It's an auction that has finished on eBay, and it shows that three people were sniping in the last two minutes before an auction closed.

This shows several snipers going at it during the end of an auction. Note the times of the bids—all bids were in the last two minutes of the auction and were similar. The best sniper won.

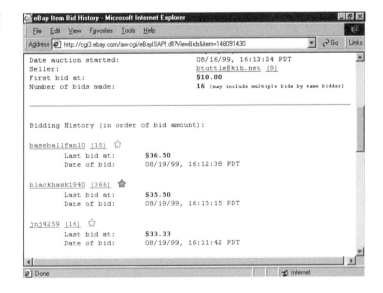

Software to Use for Power Bidding

Bidding on auction sites can be exceedingly time-consuming, and it is easy to lose track of your bidding and buying. And as you've seen, it can be nerve-wracking to snipe.

A lot of software has been developed to make it easier to bid, and there's also sniping software available to make that easier as well. Because eBay is the most popular auction site, a lot of this software was written specifically for eBay, although there's also software that works on other auction sites as well.

You can find some of this software for sale on eBay itself. But I recommend that you don't buy any auction software sight unseen. Some of the software is good; other less so; and auction software in particular is so subjective that one someone else likes, you won't. Much of the auction software is shareware, which means that you can try it out for free for a limited time before deciding whether you want to buy it. Sometimes you'll be able to download the software for free from eBay. A good thing to do is to go to a big download site on the Internet, such as the ZDNet Software Library at *www.hotfiles.com*, and download and try auction software for free before deciding to buy it. Three good pieces of auction shareware are AuctionTicker, AuctionBrowser, and AuctionTamer.

Going, Going, Gone!

Basic bidding on an auction site is easy, but becoming the best bidder possible takes work and practice. The following lists what you need to know about becoming a power bidder.

- Before you bid, set the maximum price you're willing to pay for an item and stick to it.

- Research the current going cost of an item by doing research on the Internet, at shopping sites, and at as many auction sites as possible.

- When you bid, don't bid in round numbers such as $80. Instead, add pennies to your bid, such as $80.01. In that way, you can outbid others by pennies.

- A way to pre-empt others at an auction is to bid the maximum amount you're willing to pay at the very beginning. That way, you may scare others away.

- Bidding at the end of an auction can help you get your item at the lowest possible. Sniping—bidding at the last possible second or minute—can help you get items at the lowest price, but sniping requires a good deal of effort and doesn't always work.

- Special software can help you bid on auctions and keep track of them. Much auction software is shareware, which means that you can try it before you buy it.

CHAPTER 10

Getting the Goods When You Win

You've done your homework, been a smart bidder, and you've won what you wanted at an auction. Congratulations! Now it's time to pay for the goods and get them delivered.

In this chapter, you'll learn everything that happens after the auction closes and how you'll pay for and get your goods delivered.

How You'll Find Out That You've Won

The bidding on an auction has ended, and you're the high bidder. What next?

First, you have to find out that you've won. The simplest way to see if you're a winner is to go to the auction page after the auction closes. If the auction is over, the page will tell you that. On eBay, for example, it will say "Bidding is closed for this item." The page will also have the final, winning bid for the auction and the ID of the winner. If you're lucky, (and if you've followed my bidding advice from the last chapter), the ID there is yours. You can see an example of a closed auction on eBay in the following figure.

But there's a problem with using this way to find out if you're the winner. First, you may not remember the precise closing date and time when the bidding will end. If you bid on more than one auction (which many people do), it's especially difficult to remember the closing times and dates of all your auctions.

Another problem is that it's not easy to find an auction again after it closes. For example, when an auction closes on eBay, it no longer actively shows up when people are going through the site. When you browse through categories, it won't show up. And if you do a simple search, it won't show up either. There are only a

What You'll Learn in This Chapter

▶ How to confirm information about the selling price, get the email address of the seller and similar information from the email that the auction site sends you or directly from the auction page on the site.

▶ How to contact the seller, or have the seller contact you, to make arrangements about the method of payment and how the item will be shipped.

▶ How to choose the right method of payment.

▶ How to fill out feedback about the seller after a completed transaction.

few ways to get back to the page. You can get there if you've
bookmarked it in your browser or if you remember the auction
ID. If you use the search feature that lets you search by completed
auctions, you'll be able to find it as well. Otherwise, you won't
know that you've won.

*Here's what you'll
see when you visit
an auction that's
closed on eBay.*

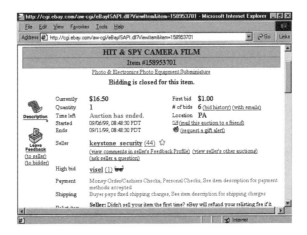

*Here's what a
closed auction
looks like on
Amazon auctions.*

Tip:
To keep track of all
your auctions, go
the advanced search
area of the auction
site and then search
on your own name
or User ID. You'll see
all the auctions in
which you're
involved.

Auction sites make it easy for you to know when you've won:
They send both you and the seller emails. The next figure shows
an example of email sent by eBay, notifying me that I've won an

auction for a Hitmonchan Pokémon holofoil card, much to the delight of my son Gabriel.

Yes, I'm the winner. Here's an email sent by eBay telling me that I've won the much-prized Hotmonchan Pokémon holofoil card.

If you're an eBay bidder, you may be confused the first time you're sent one of these emails. The subject line of the message doesn't say anything about you being a winner. It only says "eBay End of Auction" followed by the auction number and a short description of the item being auctioned. Look at the body of the message. You'll see a section titled "High-Bidder User ID." Your name will be next to that. That tells you that you've won.

There's a lot of other useful information in the email as well. It varies somewhat from site to site, but the following is the important information to look for in the email you'll get from eBay when you're a winner:

- A description of the item, plus the auction number.
- The final winning price.
- The ending date of the auction.
- The ID and email address of the winning bidder.
- The ID and email address of the seller.
- The total number of bids.
- The URL to the auction page, as well as URLs to other useful pages on eBay, such as links to follow for leaving feedback

and links to follow if you have trouble getting in touch with the seller.

After you get the winning notice, it's time to get in touch with the seller and close the deal. The seller will get the same email that you do, so he'll have your user ID and email address. You can either wait for him to contact you via email, or you can contact him yourself. Either way, you're supposed to contact each other within three business days, according to eBay terms (other auction sites may have different terms). If you try to get in touch with the seller and don't receive a response within three days of the closing of the auction, you have the right, according to eBay rules, to back out of the auction.

Manage your auction email to keep track of your winning auctions
If you get a lot of email, like I do, you run the risk of overlooking a notice that you've won an auction. There's a simple way to solve the problem—use your email's software filtering ability to automatically route winning email to a specific folder. Then check that folder at least once a day.

Most email software, like Outlook, lets you set up your own folders, so set up one named Auctions. And most email software will also let you automatically route email to a specific folder based on the sending address of the email. Check the email address from auction sites and have all that email automatically routed to your Auctions folder. In Outlook, do this by clicking the Organize button and following the instructions. If you use different email software, check how to do this there.

Getting in Touch with the Seller

After you get the official notice that you've won an auction, it's time to get in touch with the seller. The first few times you go through this, it will probably be a little bit awkward—after all, you're making a financial transaction with a complete stranger via email. And there's always the problem of whether you should immediately send email to the seller saying you want to pay for the item and be shipped the goods, or if you should wait for the seller to contact you.

For reasons I don't quite understand, the usual etiquette on eBay is that the seller often gets in touch with the bidder first rather than vice versa. The truth is, it doesn't matter who first contacts whom. If you're eager to get what you've won, send off an email to the seller.

When you win an auction, there's important information you'll need from the seller and that the seller will want from you. The following is a rundown on what's needed:

- The seller will want to know your name and address. He needs that to ship the goods to you.

- You'll both want to confirm the winning price on the auction. Don't leave it to chance or assume that each of you has thoroughly read the email from the auction site. It's best to confirm the price via email.

- You'll need the name and address of the seller—you need to know where to send your money.

- You'll need to come to terms on the method of shipping, the shipping fees, and the method of payment. Sometimes this is detailed upfront on the auction page, but not always.

- You'll want to get information on how soon the goods will be shipped to you after you send payment. This will vary according to the method of payment. If you send a check, the seller will generally wait for it to clear before sending you the goods. If you pay via money order or cashier's check, he should send them out as soon as he receives your payment.

Tip:
Consider asking the seller for his telephone number. That way, if there are any problems with the sale, you'll be able to quickly resolve the matter with a single phone call instead of a flurry of email.

Make sure to get all of these matters resolved before you pay. It's also a good idea to keep all of your email correspondence with the seller, as a reminder of what needs to be done and so you have an electronic "paper trail" in case anything goes wrong between you and the seller. You may want to create separate folders in your email program for each of your auctions so that it's easy to track all your correspondence.

What You Need to Know About Shipping Options

Sometimes a seller will offer you several different shipping options. He may offer standard shipping via priority mail, for example, for $3.00, but he may also offer you higher-priced (or lower-priced) options such as express mail or third-class mail. In general, go with normal, priority mail to save money. It will get to you within several days of its ship date, and it can be considerably less expensive than overnight shipping.

> **Consider asking that your goods be insured**
>
> Depending on the goods you're buying, it may be a good idea to ask that the buyer insure what he's sending to you. Otherwise, if the goods are damaged en route to you, you won't have any recourse. You'll have paid for the item, and there's really nothing you can do if it arrives damaged. You'll have to pay for the insurance, but it's inexpensive, usually only a dollar or so, depending on the amount of insurance purchased.
>
> Make sure to get specific insurance details from your shipper because rates and rules vary. For example, if you ship via UPS, you automatically get insurance for up to $100, but you'll have to pay extra for insurance beyond that amount. When you use the U.S. Postal Service, you get no automatic insurance—you'll have to pay for it all. Keep in mind, as well, that insurance generally covers the real market value of an item rather than the price you paid for it. So if you paid $100 for a velvet Elvis portrait, and UPS says its real market value is $4.75, you'll get the amount they set as the value.

How You'll Pay the Seller

Now comes the most uncomfortable part of the auction process—it's time to pay the seller. After all, you're sending your hard-earned money to a stranger you've never met and have never even talked to on the telephone, and you're counting on them delivering the goods after you pay.

If you've done all your pre-bidding homework, however, this really shouldn't be an issue for you. You should have checked out the seller, so you know he's trustworthy, based on other buyers' feedback. You also should know the kind of auction insurance the site carries, so you'll be covered in the unlikely event that the seller absconds with your money. The truth is, fraud on auction sites is quite rare. It can happen, though. I won't cover what to do if you suspect fraud in this chapter. For information on what to do, turn to Chapter 20, "How To Avoid Getting Burned."

In almost all instances, the seller will determine how you'll make payment. Personal checks, cashier's checks, and money orders are the most popular forms of payment, although there are other forms of payment as well—credit cards are often acceptable in the cases of auctions where you buy directly from the site. Sometimes you'll be given a choice, for example, between a money order or cashier's check. The next sections discuss what you should know about these methods of payment.

Personal Checks

Most sellers will allow you pay with a personal check, although some will accept only a money order or cashier's check. When you pay by check, there will be the greatest delay between the time you send the check and when the item will be shipped to you.

That's because the seller will wait until the check clears before sending you the goods, which can take five days or more. If you're eager to get the goods shipped to you quickly, don't pay via personal check. With other forms of payment, the seller will ship the goods as soon as he receives the money.

Just a reminder: Make sure that you have enough money in your account to cover the check. If your check bounces, the bank will charge the seller a fee, and he in turn will ask you to reimburse him. Your own bank will charge you a fee as well. In addition, you'll harm your reputation on the auction site, and you may well get negative feedback.

Money Orders

Many sellers prefer to be paid via money order rather than a personal check for one simple reason: They're as good as cash. When a seller gets a money order, he can simply deposit it in his bank account or cash it—it's the same as hard money. Because of this, the seller will ship the goods to you immediately when you pay via money order because he doesn't have to wait for the check to clear.

There's another benefit to paying by money order: You have a record of your payment that can be traced. When you buy a money order, you get a receipt that carries identifying information about the money order, so you can verify that it's been cashed and who's cashed it.

You'll have to pay a small fee for a money order, which will vary depending on where you buy it. You can get a money order at banks, the post office, and also at some retail stores (I've bought

Tip:
Be careful when filling out a money order to fill in the TO, FROM, and other fields properly. You'll also have to keep a copy of it. Ask for help, or fill it out at the counter where you can get advice.

them at my local supermarket, for example). If you get a money order from your own bank, they may offer you a reduced rate or not charge you at all.

Cashier's Checks

This one is another preferred form of payment by sellers. Like a money order, it's as good as cash, so the seller will ship you the goods within a short time after getting your cashier's check. You get cashier's checks from banks and other financial institutions.

Credit Cards

If you buy directly from the auction site itself, you'll generally be able to pay with your credit card. Additionally, because some businesses auction off goods on sites such as eBay and Amazon, you'll also be able to pay via credit card on sites like those—if you buy from a business rather than an individual.

Credit cards offer consumer protection when you pay with them, so they're a great form of payment. But don't ever send your credit card number via email to anyone. Email isn't secure, and there's a possibility that someone can snoop on it as it gets sent en route. Instead, ask for a number to call with your credit card number. Most auction sites offer secure areas where you can send your credit card safely; some businesses offer them as well.

You'll know the site is a secure one when you get a message in your browser telling you that you're entering a secure area. Depending on your browser, it will look like the following figure. Once you're at a secure site, you'll see a small icon of a locked lock at the bottom of your browser window (shown in the second following figure). If you have an older browser, the secure site may be indicated by a gold (unbroken) key instead of a locked lock. And some old or unusual browsers can't access secure sites. If you have one of these browsers, you may be directed to a non-secure site. Don't use a non-secure site for transmitting credit card information over the Internet. Instead, download the newest version of Netscape Navigator or Microsoft Internet Explorer and use that.

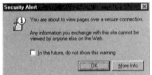

Before you enter a secure site, you'll get a message like this one.

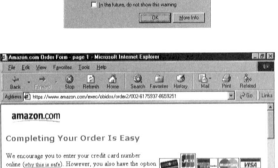

Once you enter a secure site, a little locked lock icon will appear in the bottom bar of your browser. That means it's safe to send your credit card information.

When you pay via credit card, the items will be shipped to you shortly after your payment is received and credit checked.

C.O.D.

Some buyers prefer to pay C.O.D., which stands for Cash on Delivery. That's because the item isn't paid for until it's received. (Not all sellers will agree to C.O.D. payments, though.) When you pay C.O.D., the seller tells the shipper that the item is cash on delivery. Then, when the item is delivered to the buyer, the buyer pays the shipper the cost of the item plus a C.O.D. charge. The shipper then pays the seller the cost of the item. If you're paying C.O.D., be clear ahead of time whether you or the seller will pay the extra C.O.D. fee.

Escrow Services

For big-ticket items, a good way to arrange payment is with what's called an escrow service. Escrow services ensure that you won't get burned—the seller will only get your money after you've received the goods and confirmed that they're what you were promised. The following is a summary of how escrow services work:

Don't send cash

Never pay with cash. Cash can get lost in the mail, or sellers can claim they never received payment. And sellers don't like to receive cash because there's no way to verify payment was sent or received.

1. After the buyer and seller agree to use an escrow service, the seller sends his payment to the service.

2. After the escrow service receives payment, the seller ships the item to the buyer.

3. The buyer receives the item and examines it. After he verifies it's what he was expecting, he notifies the escrow service that he's accepted it.

4. The escrow service then pays the buyer.

   In this way, the escrow service acts as a go-between and helps guarantee that you'll never get burned. If there are problems with the item, the escrow service doesn't pay the seller, and you need to return the item to him.

   Escrow services charge fees depending on the selling cost of an item. A typical fee is 5 percent of the cost of the item, with a $5 minimum fee. Several well-known escrow services are *www.iescrow.com*, *www.trade-direct.com*, and *www.tradesafe.com*.

For more information about escrow services, turn to Chapter 21, "Protecting Yourself Through Escrow Services."

How to Leave Feedback

After you've completed the buying transaction, you should leave feedback about the seller. While you're certainly not required to, you really should do it. Auction sites are based on trust and, to a great extent, are self-policing—feedback lets people know whom to deal with and whom to avoid. The only way self-policing will work is if everyone leaves feedback.

Leaving feedback is easy. There will usually be a link to a feedback form in the email that notified you that you were the winner of an auction, so just follow that. If there's no link there, go to the completed auction, and click the link there that allows you to leave feedback. (To get to the completed auction, follow the link in the email that notified you were the winner—the link will always be there.) Most auction sites have a feedback forum where you can leave feedback. To get to the eBay Feedback Forum, click Services from the main page, and then click the Feedback Forum button. On other auctions, you'll get to the feedback area differently. On Amazon, for example, click the Your Account link on the top of any auction page. When you do that, you can click a link that will show you all the auctions you've won. That page will have a link to the sellers on the auctions. To leave feedback on any seller, click the link and fill out a form.

In most feedback forums, you'll be able to say if dealing with the buyer was a positive or negative experience, and then you'll be able to add a brief comment. Pictured in the next figure is the form you fill out for leaving feedback on eBay. Then in the next figure, you can see what the completed feedback rating looks like on Amazon.

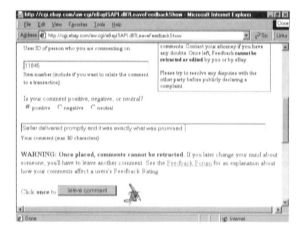

Here's how to leave feedback on eBay.

It's a good idea to leave feedback as soon as the transaction has been finished. Otherwise, you may never get around to it. And before you leave negative feedback, go through every avenue to make sure that there wasn't a misunderstanding between you and the seller and that the seller really has done something wrong. People on auction sites take negative feedback seriously, so you should be sure you're justified before leaving it.

Going, Going, Gone!

After you've won an auction, it's time to get the goods that you've won. Follow this advice for making sure that everything goes right when you win.

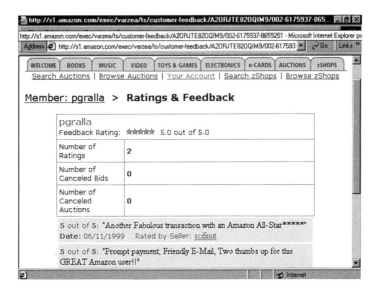

• When you win an auction, you'll be notified by email that you've won. Look at it closely to confirm that all the information is correct, and look for the email address of the seller.

• After you're been notified that you've won an auction, you'll contact the seller via email, or he'll contact you. You should arrange method of payment, how the item will be shipped to you, and confirm who will pay shipping charges.

• One of the most common ways of paying at auction sites is with a personal check. When you pay with a personal check, the seller will wait until your check clears before sending you what you've bought.

• Many sellers prefer being paid by cashier's check or money order. These are as good as cash. When you pay with either of these methods, the item will be shipped to you more quickly than when you pay with a personal check.

• When you buy directly from an auction site, you'll often pay with a credit card. Never send your credit card number via email. Only send your credit card number over a secure Internet site.

- When the transaction has been completed, make sure to fill out feedback about the seller. Auction sites are built on trust and feedback, so it's the best way to make sure that everyone prospers when bidding, selling, and buying.

CHAPTER 11

Keeping Track of Your Bidding and Buying

It's easy to lose track of all the auctions you're bidding on. After you get the hang of it, you'll find it's so simple to bid that it's easy to forget all the items you want to buy and have bid on. You certainly want to keep track of items that you're the high bidder on, so you can make sure you're not spending too much money buying at auction sites and putting a serious dent in your bank account.

In this chapter, I'll teach you how to keep track of your bidding and buying, using tools provided by auction sites and other software, as well.

Tracking Your Auctions Using Auction Search Tools

Whether you've bid only a few times on auctions, or if you're an avid auction-goer, you'll need ways to track your auction activity. Don't even try to keep track of it on paper. Take it from one who's tried; it's pretty much impossible. Use your computer to keep track of your auctions instead. In fact, the best way to track your auctions is to use the tools provided to you by the auction sites themselves. They're designed to make it easy for you to see all your auctions at a glance and to see as much detail as you want about them quickly and simply.

The way you'll do this will vary from auction site to auction site. Throughout this chapter, I'll use eBay as an example. But most auction sites have similar tools, so use the examples I show here and apply them to the auction site you're using.

What You'll Learn in This Chapter

▶ How to use the auction site's search tools to search on your user ID and see your auction activity.

▶ How to use the section of the auction site that lets you customize how you view and use the site.

▶ How to use special auction tracking software specifically designed to help you track and manage your bidding.

Using the Search Tool to Find Your Auctions

The simplest way to find all the auctions you're bidding on is to use your auction search tool. Simply go to the Search page on the site, which lets you search by a username or ID, and search on your own user ID. On eBay, for example, click the Search button on the main page. From the page that loads, go down to the Bidder Search area. Then search on your ID. The following figure shows how you do that on eBay. (For more information how to use the search feature on eBay and other sites, turn to Chapter 5, "How to Find What You Want to Buy."

Here's how you'll find all the auctions you're bidding on at eBay—go to the Bidder Search area and search on your own ID.

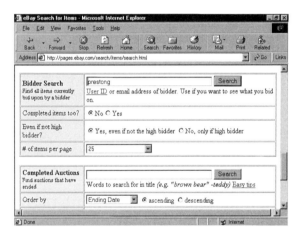

When you do this, you'll go to a page that includes all the auctions you're currently bidding on. Note that this includes *all* auctions, whether you're the high bidder or not. This means that you'll see live auctions that you've been outbid on as well as those where you're the high bidder. But this page only shows you auctions that are still live. After the auction is over, it won't show up on this page. That's because when you searched on your ID, the default was to show only current auctions.

In the next figure, you can see an example of the page that will come up when you do a search on your ID showing all your active auctions.

Note how useful this page is. For each auction, you can see if you're the high bidder, and, if not, you'll see who is. You'll see the closing time of the auction, the current high price, when the auction started, and the number identifying the auction.

Here's what you'll see when you ask to see all your active auctions on eBay.

This page does more than just let you *track* your auctions. It also serves as a jumping off point for you to visit the auctions you're bidding on—to re-bid if you're no longer the higher bidder, for example. Click the link on the item number that identifies each specific auction, and you'll be sent straight to that auction. You can now re-bid or re-examine the auction.

As you can see, this is a great way to track your current auctions. But what if you don't want to see all the auctions in which you're currently involved? What if all you want to do is see those on which you're a high bidder?

It's simple to do. Look back at the first figure in the chapter. Notice that when you search on your ID, there is a line that says, "Even If Not High Bidder?" There is a button chosen next to it labeled "Yes, Even If Not the High Bidder." That's the default for the search, and it means that it shows you all the auctions you're involved in, whether you're the high bidder or not. If you want to see only auctions that you're the high bidder on, go back to that Search page and choose the No, Only If High Bidder option.

You can also choose to see not only the current auctions you're involved in, but auctions that have closed as well. To do that, go to the search page. Notice that there's a line that says Completed Items Too and there's a button chosen next to it labeled No.

You can easily re-sort how the auctions show on the page

If you'd like to see the auctions you're bidding on in a different order than the one normally presented, it's easy to do. You can sort them by the end date of an auction, the start date, and the price.

This is particularly useful if you want to see all the auctions you're bidding on that are about to end—you'd sort them by end date. To re-sort the auctions on this page, simply click the Start Time, End Time, or Price link, and the page will reload in the new order you chose.

Simply choose Yes, and you'll see all the auctions you've been involved in bidding on, including those that have closed. The following figure shows example of a page showing completed as well as active auctions here.

You can see all the auctions you've bid on at eBay, including ones that have already closed.

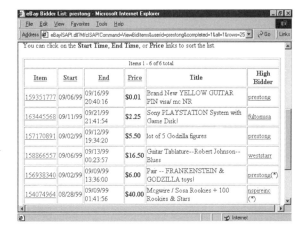

One note here: This page will only show auctions that have occurred within the last 30 days. The bidding activity on eBay is so heavy that their computers wouldn't be able to keep up with things if they had to show you past auctions as well.

The asterisk tells you who's the high bidder

On live as well as past auctions, there are asterisks next to names. The asterisk means that the person named there is the high bidder and that the auction has closed.

Using a Personalized Auction View to Track Your Bidding

Search tools are excellent ways to keep track of your bidding. But some auction sites, such as eBay and Amazon, offer even more powerful online tools to track your bidding. These tools allow you to see a customized view of the auction site. Using these tools, you can track all your bidding, your selling, and auctions and categories you haven't yet bid on but are interested in tracking from one single place.

These tools have different names on different sites, and not all sites have them. On eBay, the tool is called My eBay. On Amazon, it's called Your Auctions.

The tools generally work similarly. I'll show you how to use My eBay. In learning how to use this tool, you'll also learn how to use similar tools on other sites.

To get to My eBay, click the My eBay button on the main screen
or on almost every other screen on the site. When you do this,
you'll go to a page where you enter your ID and password. The
page also lets you customize how your My eBay area will look
and what it will display. It will let you sort your auctions in many
different ways, such as by staring price, current price, reserve
price, quantity, ending time, and many other choices. You can also
decide whether to display recent feedback about you, your
account balance, and similar information. The next figure shows
that page.

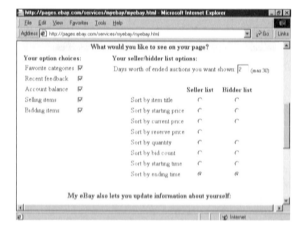

Here's how you'll customize how your My eBay area will look when you visit it.

I find it most useful to sort my auctions by ending time, which is
the default for the page. When I sort them that way, it's a
reminder to tell me when I should be visiting auctions to re-bid,
or when it's time to use sniping bidding techniques on items I
want to make sure to win. (For more information about how to
snipe, turn to Chapter 9, "Secret Techniques for Winning at
Auctions.")

There are many sections to your My eBay page. To keep track of
your auctions, go to the Items I'm Bidding On area, shown in the
following figure.

This area gives you an easy-to-scan, compact overview of all the
items you're bidding on. There's more information here than on
the search page about your auctions—it tells you how much time
is left in each auction, for example.

The My eBay area is a great way to keep track of the items you're bidding on at eBay. Many other auction sites, such as Amazon, have similar areas.

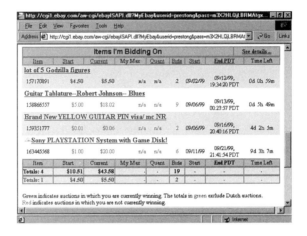

As with the page that you got when you searched on your user ID, the links here are all live, so you can jump to an auction by clicking its link. You also can re-sort the way the auctions are displayed to you by clicking the Start, Current, and other links you see.

What I find most useful about this section of My eBay is the summary information you see at the bottom. For all your auctions, you get a summary of the total amount of money bid to start the auction and the total current winning prices for the auctions. You'll see those numbers in green for each individual auction that you're currently winning.

Use a spreadsheet to track your bidding activity

Auction sites do a good job of letting you see all your bidding activity in the last 30 days. But they don't allow you to do any kind of sophisticated tracking of those auctions—such as totaling up all the money you've spent—or let you track auctions older than 30 days.

If you want a better record of your bidding activity, you'll have to keep track of it yourself. To do that, use a spreadsheet. How much of your bidding activity you'll want to track is up to you—you can get quite detailed in your analysis. But at a minimum, you should track these pieces of information for each auction in your spreadsheet:

- Item number
- Short item description
- First price you bid
- If you won
- Final bidding price

- Seller ID
- When you sent payment
- When you received goods
- Seller's email address

As I said, there's a lot more you can track as well, but you'll be in good shape if you track at least these.

Now here comes what may be the best part of this page. You can look at every single auction that you're bidding on a single page. It will be one long page that lists all the auction details, one after the other, just as if you were on an auction detail page. It's a great way to quickly see everything you want to know about every auction you're involved in. To see this page, click the See Details link.

Using Special Software for Managing Your Auctions

Because online auctions are so popular, software has been developed specifically to allow you to track and manage your auctions. There are many different kinds, but many of them will automatically go out and monitor your auctions and show you how the bidding is going. Many of them will also keep complete records of your bidding and buying.

Because eBay is so popular, there's more software for managing your auctions on eBay than on other sites. But there's software that works on other auction sites as well.

You'll find this software for sale at eBay and other auction sites. But, as with software that helps you do bidding and sniping, I recommend that you don't buy this software sight unseen. Much of this software is shareware, so you can try it out for free for a time before you decide whether to buy it or not. Sometimes you can download the software for free from the auction sites. Another good thing to do is go to an Internet download site, such as the ZDNet Software Library at www.hotfiles.com, and download and try auction software from there. For eBay only, try out AuctionTicker at www.blackthornesw.com/Bthome/ and AuctionBrowser at www.auction-browser.com/. For other auctions (and for eBay as well), try out Auction Alert at www.acubid.com.

Here's how AuctionTicker keeps track of your auction activity on eBay.

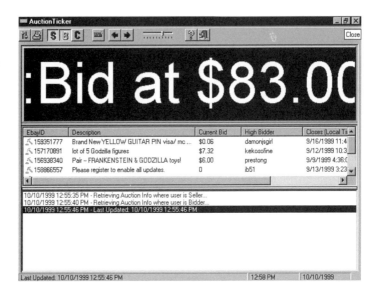

Going, Going Gone!

It's easy to lose track of all the bidding you're doing an auctions that you're the high bidder on, especially if you do a lot of bidding at auctions. But there are easy ways to keep track of your auctions. The following is a summary of how to keep track of them:

- Use your auction site's search tools to find all the auctions you're bidding on—search on your user ID and review the results.

- From the results you receive, you can visit all of your auctions. To do that, click the links and you can go to each.

- For a more powerful way to track your auction activity, use the section of the auction site that lets you view personalized information about your activity. On eBay, it's called My eBay, and it's called Your Auctions on Amazon. For other auction sites, see what it's called.

- If you want to track your bidding and buying over the long-term to do calculations on it, create a spreadsheet to track your auction activity.

- You can buy special software designed specifically for tracking your auction activity. Much of this software is shareware, which means that you can try it before you buy it. Get the software from auction sites or an Internet download site, such as *www.hotfiles.com.*

PART 3

Auction Marketing 101

CHAPTER 12

Creating Your First Auction

You've got something you want to sell, and you believe the world wants to buy it. Online auctions offer one of the world's easiest ways to sell with a minimum of effort.

In this chapter, I'll teach you how to create your first auction listing. You'll learn how to do everything from choosing a title and category to writing a description, choosing the right bidding price, and more. By the end of the chapter, you'll have learned how to create a listing, and you'll see it live online.

Step One: Decide on a Selling Price

So you've got an item you're ready to sell. That's good. Get ready to make some money.

Before you do anything, you have to decide something very basic: For how much should you sell your item?

To determine that, you should do some basic research, both on the auction site itself as well as on the rest of the Internet. In Chapter 7, "Buyer's Checklist: What to Do Before Making a Bid," I taught you how to research the price of any item you were interested in buying. The same advice holds true to research the price of something you're interested in selling. The following is a summary of how to determine the right selling price; turn to Chapter 7 for more details.

- *Search the Internet for the cost of an item*—Use Internet search engines such as *www.yahoo.com* and *www.lycos.com* to get all the information available about the item you're planning on selling, including related Web sites that include selling prices and similar information.

What You'll Learn in This Chapter

- ▶ How to determine your minimum bidding price.

- ▶ How to choose the best title and the proper category.

- ▶ How to write an accurate, detailed description.

- ▶ How to choose a variety of options, such as paying extra for special placement, to spice up your auction.

- ▶ How to set auction length, minimum bid, and other last-minute auction details.

- ▶ How to review your auction listing to make sure it's accurate.

- ▶ How to post your listing online and view it online while you wait for bids.

- *Search online shopping sites for selling prices*—If what you're selling is new, or only slightly used, and isn't a collectible, see what the item is selling for at online shopping sites. That'll help you determine what the going price should be at your auction.

- *See what the item or similar items are selling for on your auction site*—Using your auction site's search tools, search auctions for identical or similar items. When you do this, make sure to search for completed auctions—that's the only way you'll know the true current selling price. If you search for auctions that are still active, you won't be able to see the final selling price.

Search multiple auction sites

To search many auction sites simultaneously, head to *www.biddersedge. com, www. auctionwatch.com,* and *www. auctionrover.com.* You can search for items using them, and they report on auctions selling them at many sites. They don't search all auction sites, so check which ones they don't search.

- *See what the item is selling on other auction sites*—To get the most accurate selling price for your item, look on other auction sites, not just the one on which you're planning to auction it.

When you do all this, you'll get a good sense of what your item should generally sell for. Based on that, you should decide whether to set a minimum bid—a minimum price bidders have to meet if they want to bid. You can also set a "reserve" price on the item. It's a price you set—and that only you know—below which you're not required to sell the item.

Note that you can set your public minimum bid lower than your privately known reserve price. You might do that if you want a certain minimum for the item and want to test the waters to see if you can get a higher price. If the higher reserved price isn't reached, you still have the option of selling the item. For more information about reserve price auctions, go back to Chapter 3, "Understanding Auction Basics."

Step 2: Choose Your Item's Title and Category

When you know how much you plan to sell your item for, it's time to create your auction. The way you do it differs somewhat from site to site, but it's generally similar. In this chapter, I'll walk you through the steps and show you how to create your auction on eBay. Check how to do it at different auction sites.

We'll take a real-life example. I'm going to create an auction to
sell two pieces of shrink-wrapped educational software I was
given but for which I have no need: *Virtual Physics: Escape from
Braindeath* and *Virtual Physics: The Eggs of Time*. I'll show you
how to do it step-by-step on eBay. You can apply the same methods to other auction sites as well.

To start on eBay, click the Sell button on the main page. When
you do that, you'll go Sell Your Item page, shown in the following figure. (To enter an auction using this page, you'll have to be
registered with eBay. If you haven't registered yet, now's the
time.)

On other auction sites, such as Amazon and Yahoo!, you start off
similarly. Shown after the eBay picture is how you start creating a
new listing on Amazon.

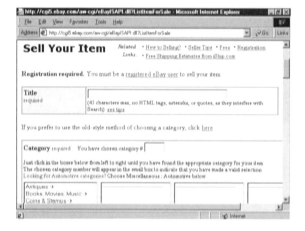

Get ready to
make some
money. Here's the
start of the form
you'll fill out on
eBay to create an
auction.

Start out by filling out the title. This may be the single most
important thing you'll do to make sure your item sells. There are
literally millions of items for sale out there. If your auction does-
n't have a title that's both clear and catches people's attention,
you won't sell your item, or, if you do, it'll be for less money that
it otherwise would have. To make matters more difficult, you have
a maximum of 45 characters to say it in, including spaces and
punctuation.

Here's how you fill out a form on Amazon to create a new auction.

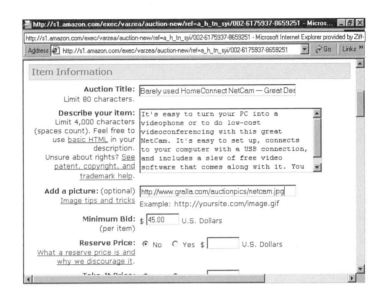

For my software, I used a title of "VIRTUAL PHYSICS TWO PACK—COOL AND USEFUL!!" I used capitalization, because that draws more attention. On auction sites, unlike the rest of the Internet, capitalization isn't considered a breech of etiquette. Everyone does it. In fact, it's almost expected.

Keep in mind that people will be searching on your title

The title you use for your auction listing will be used when someone is doing a search on the auction site. Make sure that all the most important keywords are in the description so it can be found by searchers.

There's a lot more to learn about how to write proper titles. For more help, turn to Chapter 13, "How to Write Effective Ad Copy."

Next, choose the category. Again, take care here. If you don't categorize it properly, people won't find it. You want the category to be broad enough so that the most people will find it, but narrow enough so that when people find it as they browse, it'll be just the kind of item they're looking for in that particular category.

Choosing a category is easy on eBay. In the category area, click on the category that best describes your item in the left-most pane. As you do that, a list of subcategories will appear. Click the closest subcategory and an even more specific subcategory will appear. Keep clicking this way until your final subcategory is chosen. The next figure shows you how to choose a subcategory.

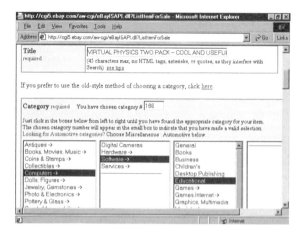

Here's how to choose the proper subcategory for your auction on eBay. Just keep clicking until you get to the proper one.

Step Three: Write the Description

OK, now here's the hardest part for most people: Writing a description of what they're selling. You need to be as descriptive as possible, so that bidders have as complete an understanding of what's for sale as possible. But you also have to do a bit of selling here, to give bidders a reason to want to buy, and you don't want to mislead in any way.

Be as complete as you can when describing the item, this is an instance when more is definitely better. Because bidders can't physically examine the goods you're selling, they're going to spend a lot of time reading your words. Take care to use words that describe the physical condition of what you're selling, such as poor, fair, good, new, and so on. (Again, be absolutely accurate here, don't try to shade the truth in your favor or you'll have some very unhappy buyers and you'll get a bad reputation as well.)

You can use HTML coding in your descriptions

Most auction sites, such as eBay, allow you to use HTML when you put together your descriptions of the item you have for sale. HTML is the language of the Web and lets you use different fonts, colors, add backgrounds, pictures, graphics, and more. Auctions that use HTML are much more eye-catching and appealing than plain text auctions. But if you go crazy adding too many fonts, pictures, and colors, you'll turn off potential bidders. For more information about how to use HTML to create an auction, turn to Chapter 14, "HTML for Auctioneers."

There's an art to putting together the best description possible of your auction. For more details, see Chapter 13.

The following is the description I put together or selling my software:

> Do your kids from grades six through nine want to learn every-thing about physics? You can learn about waves, Newton' Laws, machines, thermodynamics, magnetism, optics and much more with these two unopened shrink-wrapped programs for the PC: *Virtual Physics, The Eggs of Time* and *Virtual Physics, Escape from Braindeath.* Kids can do 3D experiments and immerse themselves in an interactive world where learning is fun. This software has been endorsed by Professor William Goddard of Caltech. The two programs have a retail value of $59.95. If you have any questions, simply email me. Thanks for bidding, and good luck. Seller pays for shipping.

By the way, the auction was a success and drew a good number of bidders.

Step Four: Choose Extra Options for Spicing Up Your Auction

After you've finished the description on eBay, you'll be able to choose from a variety of options to spice up your auction. Again, many other auction sites will have similar options to these, and they work pretty much the same. Check those sites for the details of how to choose their special options. The following are the extra options you can choose on eBay and what you need to know about each when putting together an auction:

- *Picture URL*—You can add a picture to your auction. As the saying goes, a picture is worth a thousand words, and pic-tures help sell your item. For this chapter, we'll leave this entry blank, so no picture will appear. I've devoted an entire chapter to handling pictures, Chapter 15, "A Picture's Worth a Bigger Bid," so turn there for more details about how to handle pictures on auction sites.

- *The Gallery*—The Gallery is a special area on eBay that allows people to browse auctions by looking at thumbnail pictures. You can only be part of the Gallery if you've included pictures in your auction. It costs only 25 cents to be part of the Gallery, so if you include a picture of your item, this one's a no-brainer. You can also pay $19.95 to have your item featured in the Gallery, for greater visibility. Only pay extra if you have a big-ticket item you want to sell.

- *Boldface title*—If you pay extra ($2 on eBay), you can have your listing appear in bold. Unless you're selling a very low-cost item (in which case the two dollars will eat into your profit) it may be two dollars well-spent because it draws more attention to your item.

- *Featured*—On eBay, as on other auction sites, you can pay extra to have the auction featured for a time on the front page of the site. On eBay, you pay $99.95 and the item appears for as long as it's being sold in the featured auctions section of the site. Some auctions are randomly selected from the featured auctions section to appear on the front page. Use this feature only if you have a big-ticket item for sale; otherwise it won't be worth the cost.

- *Featured in category*—You can choose to have your item featured in a category instead of on eBay's front page (the same is true of other auction sites). This gets you less visibility than the front page of the entire site, but more visibility than most other auctions. It'll cost you $14.95 on eBay. Again, only do this if you're selling a relatively big-ticket item.

- *Great gift icon*—If what you're selling would make a good gift for someone, you can pay one dollar on eBay to have a gift icon appear next to the listing. For gift-type items, especially near a holiday, this is a good bet.

Step Five: Choose the Auction Length, Minimum Bid, and Other Final Details

After ,you've chosen the options for spicing up your auction on eBay, you'll choose the final details, such as the auction length and minimum bid. Again, the way you'll do it on other auction sites may differ from how you do it on eBay, but the rules you'll follow will generally be the same on most auction sites. In this section, I'll teach you how to do it. The following figure shows many of these final details filled in on an eBay auction listing page.

It's getting very near the end: Filling in many of the final details on the page that lets you create an auction on eBay.

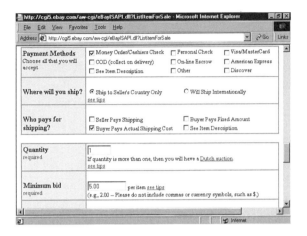

Set the Bidding Price

Earlier in this chapter, I taught you how to determine a minimum bidding price for your auction and to decide whether to set a reserve price. On eBay, scroll to near the bottom of the page for creating your auction, and you'll see where to set these prices. Be careful when using reserve auctions, you'll pay eBay the same price whether your item sells or not. On normal auctions, you only pay the auction site a minimal fee for creating an auction if your item sells. Later in this chapter, I'll explain auction sites' pricing structures.

On eBay, and on many other auction sites, the minimum bidding price you set determines the minimum bidding increment. So if you set a minimum bid of $1, for example, the minimum bidding increment is 25 cents; if you set a minimum bid of $5, the minimum bidding increment is 50 cents. The higher the minimum bid, the more money you'll get for each subsequent bid.

Don't forget to include your location

Every auction on eBay requires that you include your location, including your city or town, state, and ZIP code. If you don't include this information, eBay won't allow the auction to go online.

When setting your minimum bid,, balance drawing people in against making sure you get a fair price for what you're selling. A low minimum price will draw more bidders, but then each subsequent bid will be not much higher than the minimum bid. A higher minimum price will scare away bidders, but then each subsequent bid will be a larger jump above the minimum bid.

In our example, I'm not going to set a reserve price. I'll set a minimum bidding price of $5, because I want to make sure I get at least that much money for the software, and because I'm hoping several bidders will bid up the price.

Set the Length of the Auction

Another detail that you need to determine: How long should your auction last? A common length is a week—different auction sites let you set different amounts of time. On eBay, for example, you have a choice of setting your auction for three, five, seven, or ten days. Later in this book, in Chapter 16, "Secret Tips for Creating Auctions That Sell," I'll give you tips and advice on how to decide how long your auction should be. For the purposes of completing the form on eBay now, we'll leave it at the eBay default of seven days.

Set Shipping and Payment Options

Next up: Set your shipping and payment options. First, decide who pays for shipping. This one's simple: The buyer should. On just about any auction you come across, sellers pay, and there's no reason at all your should diverge from that general rule. On eBay, you can decide to specifically say how much shipping will cost, or you can simply say that the buyer will pay the shipping costs, whatever they turn out to be. Unless you know the precise shipping costs, it's a good idea to merely say that the buyer will pay whatever the shipping costs turn out to be. That's what we'll do in our example.

When it comes to accepting payment, the simpler the better. Money orders and cashier's checks are as good as cash, and that's my preferred method of accepting payment. You can also decide to accept personal checks, but you'll have to wait longer for them to clear—and there's always the issue of what happens if a check bounces. However, many people like to pay by personal check. In this auction, we'll say that payment is via cashier's check or money order.

Keep in mind that if you limit the payment options and don't accept personal checks (and if you also limit the shipping methods), you'll be cutting down on the number of potential bidders. Fewer bidders can mean a lower selling price. You'll have to balance your desire for tried-and-true payment methods versus the total number of people who might want to bid.

Set Other Miscellaneous Options

There's just a few more options you'll need to set for finishing your first auction on eBay or other sites. Enter how many items you have to sell. In our instance, we have one. If you want it to be a private auction, click that option.

Step Six: Review Your Auction Listing

After you've filled out the form on the auction site, you should review your listing before actually placing it. To do this on eBay, click the Review button at the bottom of the page. You'll then get a chance to review your listing by looking at a page like the one shown in the next figure. Other auction sites have different ways of reviewing your listing, but they'll all let you review it before posting it.

Here's where you'll review your auction listing on eBay to make sure that everything is as you like it.

Pay careful attention to all the details here, it's the last chance you'll have to make sure everything is right before the world starts bidding. Pay special attention to the fees you're being charged, and make sure they're exactly what you expect them to be.

Figure What You'll Be Charged for Your Auction Listing

Just before you're going to post your listing is a good time to figure out what you'll be charged for an auction listing.

The price varies depending on the auction site, the options you've chosen for listing your auction, and how much money you're charging for your item. On eBay, however, you're charged a listing fee, called an *insertion fee*, for each item you auction. The fee is based on the minimum bid you set. For items for which you set a minimum bid of under $10, you're charged 25 cents; for items between $10 and $24.99, you're charged 50 cents; for items between $25 and $49.99, you're charged $1; and for items $50 and over, you're charged $2.

In addition to the insertion fee, there are a variety of fees you could be charged, depending on whether you've decided to add boldface to your listing, whether you want you auction featured, and similar options. I covered those earlier in the chapter.

Finally, if your item sells, you'll be charged a percentage of the selling price. If your item sells for $25 or less, you pay 5 percent of the selling cost. If your item sells for between $25 and $1,000, you'll be charged 5 percent of the first $25, plus 2.5 percent of the amount over $25. If you're lucky enough to sell an item for over $1,000, you'll be charged all that, plus 1.25 percent of the selling price over $1,000.

There are a variety of ways you can pay eBay and other auction sites, including credit cards, personal checks, or money orders. Most auction sites, though, won't accept cash. Check the exact details on your site's area that details how to sell your items.

Step Seven: Post Your Listing

After you've reviewed your auction listing, and everything is as it should be, it's time to take the plunge and press the button. On eBay, go to the bottom of the auction review page, and click Submit My Listing. You've done it! You'll get a verification that your auction has started, as shown in the following figure. The verification will look different on other auction sites.

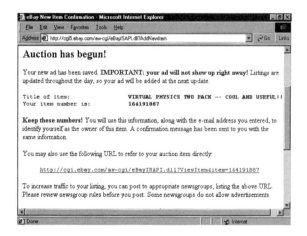

It may take a little while for the auction to show up on eBay, by the way, but the site is updated throughout the day, so the delay should be a short one. In general, the same holds true of other auction sites.

As you can see in the preceding figure, you'll get an item number. Copy it down for future reference and so you can always get back to the auction. There will also be a link you can click to go to your auction. Click it now. You want to absolutely verify that the auction is exactly the way you want it. When you do, you'll go to your auction page and see it as the rest of the world will. The following figure shows the completed auction.

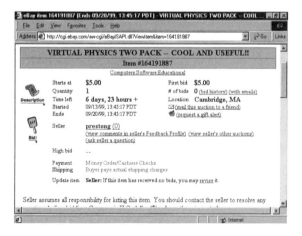

Check every aspect of your completed auction. It's easy to over-look things on forms, and this is the first time you'll see it the way the world sees it. If you find any errors, you may have time to fix them. If no bids have come in—and they shouldn't have because you created the auction only moments ago, and it proba-bly isn't visible yet—you can still correct them. To fix any errors, go to the Update area and click where it says, Seller: If This Item Has Received No Bids, You May Revise It. You'll then go to a page that lets you correct any errors.

Shortly after creating an auction, you'll get a notice telling you that your auction has been made live and giving you all the vital information about the auction. Keep that email for future reference.

Going, Going, Gone!

It's easy to create an auction listing. Just follow this advice and you'll do it quickly and easily.

- Before starting to create your auction listing, determine the minimum bidding price by researching how much similar items have sold for at auctions and by checking online shop-ping sites and related Web sites.

- When choosing a title for your item, be sure that it's clear and catches people's attention. Also keep in mind that when people search auction sites for items, they'll search through your description, so make sure that it has keywords on which people might search. Some sites also let you pay extra to have your listing in boldface. Unless you're selling a very low-priced item, it's worthwhile to pay the extra money.

- When you choose a category, it should be broad enough to bring in as many bidders as possible, but narrow enough so that it will draw focused bidders.

- The item description should be as detailed as possible and should describe the general condition of the item. Make sure to be honest as to its condition. Try also to make your description as enticing as possible to draw in bidders. Under no circumstances, however, should you stretch the truth as a way to get people to bid.

- On many sites, including eBay, you can pay extra to get your auction listing put in special areas of the site or to draw attention to it in other ways. This can be very expensive, so only do this if you are selling a relatively high-cost item.

- When creating your auction listing, have the buyer be responsible for shipping charges. For payment, money orders and cashier's checks are as good as cash, so they're excellent ways to accept payment.

CHAPTER 13

How to Write Effective Ad Copy

There are millions of auctions taking place every day on eBay. That means that there are millions of auctions competing with yours for bidders' attention.

So how do you make sure that bidders and buyers come to your auctions? Write effective auction copy—titles and listings that catch their attention and get them competing with each other to buy what you have for sale. In this chapter, you'll learn how to write the most effective auction copy so you'll create auction listings that give you the best chance to sell your goods.

Use Eye-Catching Titles

Perhaps the single most important thing you can do to help make sure that you sell your items for the most possible money is to write an eye-catching title. As people browse through auction listings, that's all they're going to see—your auction's title. If your title doesn't catch their eyes, and if doesn't include specific, accurate information about what you're selling, you won't hook the buyers.

Follow these tips to write a title that draws in buyers:

- *Don't use unnecessary words*—Pare down the title until it's as brief as possible. Every word should matter and convey important information.

- *Use words that draw attention to your auction*—Words in titles like "rare'" or "beautiful" draw immediate attention. Use them—but only if they're true.

- *Use abbreviations commonly found on auction sites*—There's a limit on how many characters you can use at auction sites.

What You'll Learn in This Chapter

- ▶ Techniques for writing titles that catch potential bidders' attention.

- ▶ How to make sure that your auctions will be found by searchers as well as browsers.

- ▶ All the different ways you can write descriptions that get people to place their bids.

- ▶ The four essential things that should be part of every auction listing.

Titles are also used when people search through auction sites

The words in titles are used when people search an auction site. So the title should include as many descriptive keywords as possible. That way, your auction will be found by the most people.

On eBay, for example, you have a limit of 45 characters, including spaces. Study the titles of auctions in your categories to see what abbreviations are commonly used. For example, you can use N/R or No Res to mean no reserved price, 14K instead of 14 carat gold, and 17C to mean seventeenth century.

- *Use the proper acronyms when selling collectibles*—There's a whole language of acronyms you can use when selling collectibles, such as NRFB, which means "never removed from box." Study the category of item that you're selling to learn which abbreviations to use. Be careful, though, not to use abbreviations for the most important words in your auction title, such as BK for book. If you did that, people searching on the word book wouldn't find your auction.

- *Avoid using special keyboard characters*—Every auction site is filled with titles and words that have special keyboard characters in them, like L@@K!!!! Avoid them. They're so overused that people pass right over them.

- *Point out what's unique or special about what you're selling*—Do you have a one-of-a-kind item or one in mint condition? Is it a particular brand or model number that is in great demand? Think of what sets your item apart from the mass of other auction items out there, and make sure that comes across in the title. To see what I mean, look at the following figure from Yahoo! auctions. The first listing, "Elvis With Guitar...Life Size Cutout!!! GREAT FOR XMAS," does a great job of explaining what's special about the item. By way of contrast, the second listing, "Elvis Plaque," does a terrible job—you don't know what's unique or interesting about the plaque from the title.

- *Pay extra for a bold-faced listing*—Bold face draws attention to your listing. You won't pay much extra to have your title appear in bold face on most sites. (On eBay, for example, it only cost two extra dollars.) It's money well spent.

Elvis With Guitar... Life Size Cutout!!! GREAT FOR XMAS	$34.77	-	3 hrs
Elvis Plaque	$6.99	-	3 hrs
Rare Moments With The King - Elvis Presley VHS	$5.99	-	3 hrs
King of Music Clock	$17.99	2	3 hrs
Young Elvis - Elvis Presley VHS	$5.99	-	3 hrs
ELVIS CLOCK...a perfect Christmas gift for Elvis fans...	$39.95	17	3 hrs
Awesome Elvis Presley button!	$5.95	1	4 hrs
ELVIS in Star 20th Anniversary Death Issue	$6.00	-	4 hrs
Elvis-plate-the Super - Star-no Reserve!!!	$26.50	-	4 hrs
Unique Elvis Goldtone Identification Bracelet Bonus	$7.77	-	4 hrs
elvis world by jane and michael stern 210 page some un seen befor pictures mint	$50.00	-	4 hrs
ELVIS In Concert 1977 & Bonus Tour'77 Video!	$24.95	-	4 hrs
Elvis The Last TourThe Best of 1977 Import Video	$24.95	-	4 hrs
Elvis In Concert!!!3 Pice Set Aug 16 1997 Rare	$21.77	-	5 hrs

The top listing on this Yahoo! auction page does a great job of pointing out what's unique about the item, while the second listing falls flat.

- *Don't stretch the truth*—In your attempt to draw in buyers, you may feel compelled to stretch the truth to make your item sound more appealing or more unique than it really is. Avoid doing that. If you promise more than your auction delivers, you'll only annoy potential buyers who will avoid your auctions in the future. And once you get a bad reputation on an auction site, it's hard to live down.

How to Write Descriptions That Sell

If you've done your job right, the title will be enough of a draw for potential bidders to get to your auction page. Good work—you've done the job right. But that's only the beginning. Now you need people to actually bid and buy. The title is like a pleasing storefront display that brings people into the store. After they come into the store, there need to be displays and goods so that they're enticed to buy what you have to sell.

In the same way that a store needs to be appealing and its goods put nicely on display, your description needs to be laid out nicely and clearly, and it needs to be enticing enough so that people want to buy what you're selling.

Follow this advice, and you'll go a long way toward writing the best descriptions to help sell your items at auctions:

- *Be comprehensive in your description*—The more details you provide, the more likely someone is to bid on what you have up for sale. Make sure to list all of the item's features, especially anything that makes it unique. You're not limited in how much space you use for your description, so feel free to use the space.

- *Be enthusiastic in your description*—If you're not excited about the item you have for sale, how do you think the bidder will feel? You want to impart a sense of enthusiasm and energy in the description that you write.

- *Accurately portray the condition of the item that you're selling*—Don't try to hide the fact that your item has flaws or defects, or that it's been used. The buyer will find out the truth, and, if you've been inaccurate in your portrayal of the item, may ask for his money back. In any event, you're more likely than not get negative feedback. On the other hand, don't dwell solely on the item's defects—you mainly want to point out what's good about it.

- *Stress the benefits of the item you're selling, not just its features*—Let's say you're selling a Palm digital organizer. If you were going to stress only its features, you might say, "Comes with 2 MB RAM." That's not much of a sell. If, instead, you say, "It will store your entire yearly schedule, address book, all your To-Do Lists, your expense accounts, and more in its 2 MB of RAM," you're stressing its specific benefits. You're more likely to get bidders when you can sell them on the benefits of the item you have for sale.

- *Start off your description with a bang*—If you don't grab potential bidders in your first sentence, you're going to lose them. That's the time to stress the benefits of what you have for sale, its uniqueness, its special features, and anything else you can think of that will get people to want to buy it.

You can link from your description to other Web pages

For some items, particularly specialty items or collectibles, you may have a great deal of informational material available. But, while you want to be comprehensive in your listing, you don't want to force potential bidders to scroll through page after page after page of details.

There's an easy way to solve the problem: You can link to another Web page from an auction listing. You can put more detailed information about the item for sale on your personal Web page. For information on how to link to other Web pages, turn to Chapter 14.

- *End your description with a summing-up sales pitch*—The last words of a listing can be the primary thing that people remember after reading your listing, and it's probably the last thing they'll read before making a bid. Because of that, you want to make sure that the end of your description sums up the item and stresses all its benefits with enthusiasm.

- *Anticipate questions that potential buyers may have about the item*—Stand back for a moment and imagine yourself as a buyer of what you have for sale. What questions do you think they'd ask about it, what more might they want to know? Ask yourself that, and then include the answers in your description.

- *Include brand names, manufacturer, years of manufacture, and other similar information*—There are collectors out there who collect everything imaginable. You may not realize it, but collectors may specialize in the precise brand or manufacturer of what you have for sale. It's important to include these details in your descriptions.

Look at the following figure from Amazon auctions, you'll see a well-written description that takes into account many of these tips.

This description
from Amazon auc-
tions does all the
right things: It has
a great sales
pitch, accurately
describes the
item, uses vivid
descriptions, and
makes people
want to buy.

This beautiful **'32 Pontiac** "static model"
is handcarved from rich walnut and maple woods

Master carver, Joe Montagno,
is well known for his "replica stagecoaches"
which he was commissioned by Wells Fargo Co. to build.

These handcrafted wooden masterpieces are on display
at the historic San Fernando Mission, in California
and also at the bank's executive offices in Los Angeles.

Joe Montagno's **'32 Pontiac** measures approx. 8.0" long, 3.5" wide, and 3" tall.
A "Collector's Piece", Signed and dated by the artist!

Five Things to Include in Every Auction Listing

If you write eye-catching titles and write descriptions that sell,
you'll go a long way toward making sure that your item gets bid
on and bought. But there's more advice you should follow as
well. You should include the following five things in every auction listing, without fail:

Sellers should
check their email
frequently

If you're going to
encourage bidders
to email you with
questions, you
should check your
email several times a
day and respond
promptly to ques-
tions. Otherwise,
you'll lose bidders
and the sale.

- *Tell people they should email you with questions or for more
  information*—If people feel that you're open to answering
  questions, they'll be more likely to trust you, and will be
  more likely to bid. If someone takes the time to email a question to you, it means you've piqued their interest and are
  more likely to make a sale.

- *Include details about shipping, insurance, and payment*—You
  want to leave no questions in the bidder's mind about how
  the transaction will work. Giving precise details like this will
  put them at their ease so they know exactly what to expect.

- *Describe your expertise, if any, in the category of the thing
  you're selling*—Are you an expert in depression glass? A collector of Nancy Ann dolls? If you have special expertise or
  are a collector of what you're selling, let people know that,

and then tell them why you value the item you're selling. Not only will it lend an authoritative voice to your auction, but other collectors will feel a kind of kinship with you and will be more likely to bid. You may also gain new friends with common interests in this way.

The following figure, from Amazon auctions, is a great example of an excellently written description, taking into account many of the tips in this chapter. The autographed photo is described fully, even including the color of the ink used to sign it. The seller is clearly enthusiastic about the worth of the item, plays up his expertise as a long-time collector, and includes information on how to track the authenticity of the item. It's clear that the buyer will pay for shipping. If you're selling at an auction, it's a great description to use as a model.

Look at this excellent example of a description of an item, and see how frequently it follows the advice found in this chapter.

Promoting your auction outside the auction site will help bring in buyers

Don't be shy about letting the world know about your auction. You don't have to sit back and wait for people to come to the auction site and bid. Instead, you can tell people outside the auction site about your auction and invite them in. If you have a personal Web page, put links to your auctions there. If you correspond with people via email, put links

continues

continued

to your auctions there as well. You can also go to public discussion areas on the Internet, such as newsgroups, and publicize your auctions. Just make sure, before posting a public notice about your auction, that the rules of the newsgroup or discussion area don't ban commercial solicitations.

- *Thank potential bidders for their interest*—Your mother was right: manners count. They especially count online when you're anonymous and faceless. Thanking people in your auction listing will make them feel that you're trustworthy and likable—and they'll be more likely to bid.

Going, Going, Gone!

One of the best ways to make sure your item sells is to write effective auction copy. You need to write catchy titles and descriptions that sell and are completely accurate.

- Keep auction titles as pithy as possible, but make sure that you include all relevant keywords so that people will find them when searching as well as browsing.

- Use descriptive words like "rare" to draw attention to your auction listing, and point out any distinctive characteristics of what you have for sale.

- In both your title and description, don't stretch the truth— accurately portray your item's condition. If you mislead buyers, they may want to return the item and will give you negative feedback.

- When writing your auction description, be as complete as possible, going into as much detail as you can describing the item. Pay particular attention to describing what's unique about it and why it's worth buying.

- When you write descriptions, stress the benefits of the item you're selling, not just its features.

- Remember to let potential bidders know that they can contact you via email, and thank them in the description for their interest in your item.

CHAPTER 14

HTML for Auctioneers

One of the quickest ways to make an item sell is to dress up your auction—make it stand out from the crowd—and use it to most effectively convey just how good a deal people are getting if they bid on your item.

To do that, you'll use HTML (Hypertext Markup Language), the language of the Web. It's not that hard to learn the basics of HTML—in fact, it's so easy that anyone can do it. You'll be able to use HTML to create eye-catching auctions with special fonts, headlines, graphics, and more, and to make it more likely to sell your items at a higher price than you otherwise would have.

In this chapter, I'll teach you how to use HTML to dress up your auctions and create auctions that sell. You'll learn the basics of HTML and a variety of HTML commands for creating eye-catching Web pages.

The Basics of HTML

HTML is the language that tells Web browsers how to display Web pages. Fancy fonts, big headlines, graphics—all of that and more is done by the use of HTML. When you go to a Web page, your browser looks at the HTML and then displays it to you, following the HTML instructions embedded in the Web page.

HTML pages themselves are simple pages of text, with special instructions—called *tags*—that tell the browser how to display the page. As you'll learn in this chapter, it's not that hard to learn how to use these tags to make better-looking auction pages.

The most basic thing to know about HTML is that the tags are enclosed within brackets. Each tag has an instruction to do a particular thing, such as displaying text at a certain size, displaying it as bold or italic, or displaying a graphic. Usually, tags contain a pair of instructions—the first one turns on the action, and the second one turns it off.

What software you'll need to create Web pages

There are many tools you can use to create Web pages, including special HTML editors. For what you'll do for auctions, however, the simplest tool to use is Windows Notepad or another simple text editor. Start the program and create a file using HTML codes as outlined in this chapter. Then save the file to your hard drive using an *.html* extension. For example, you could save the file with the name of *myauction.html*.

To preview your work, start your browser. Then use its Open command to open the file you just created. You'll be able to see your HTML page as it will appear in your auction.

Let's take an example. Say you want to make text on a page bold-faced. You'd put the tag *<B>* in front of the text you'd want to make bold, and the tag *</B>* after the text you'd want to make bold, as shown in the following:

<B>This is boldfaced text</B>

The first tag is called the *start tag*, and the second tag is called the *end tag*. You'll notice that the / is used as a way to turn off the formatting. Note that any text you don't put tags around defaults to plain Times Roman text.

There are hundreds of tags you can use like this on HTML pages, but you won't need to know them all to create auction pages. In fact, you'll only need to know a very few basic ones. In the rest of this chapter, I'll teach you the most important tags you'll need to know for creating eye-catching Web pages.

How to Format Text and Create Headlines

Auction pages are mainly made up of text. So the most important HTML commands you can learn are commands that format text in a variety of ways, most notably ways that can help you make headlines and use boldfaced text. The following are the most important text-formatting commands and what they do:

<H1>This makes the biggest headline</H1>

<H2>This makes the second biggest headline</H2>

<H3>This makes the third biggest headline</H3>

(You can choose from six different sized headlines. For the fourth, fifth, and sixth sized headlines, just substitute their numbers in the start and end tags.)

<H>This makes the text bold</H>

<I>This italicizes the text</I>

<U>This underlines text</U>

<CENTER>This centers text</CENTER>

<TT>This creates typewriter-style text(also called monospaced)</TT>

<P>This inserts a blank line and starts a new paragraph</P>

You can combine these tags with each other as well. For example, to have the biggest headline text centered in the page, you'd use the following code:

<CENTER> <H1>Big Centered Headline</H1></CENTER>

Let's take what we just learned and use it to create HTML for a simple auction listing. We're going to use two levels of centered headlines, boldfaced text, normal text, and centered italicized text:

<CENTER><H1>One-Time Offer!</H1></CENTER>

<CENTER><H2>Two Mint Condition Godzilla Posters</H2></CENTER>

<B>Godzilla, King of the Monsters!</B> Godzilla shoots flames out of his mouth, destroying Tokyo.

<P>

<B>It's Alive!</B>Godzilla strides through a river, breaking a bridge in two.

<P>

I've had these two posters since I was a child and the first Godzilla movie came out. They're in perfect condition and are ideal for any true Godzilla lover.

<P>

<CENTER><I>I accept cashier's checks and money orders. Buyer pays handling and shipping</I></CENTER>

Don't use blinking text

HTML includes an incredibly annoying tag that makes text blink on and off. You use it like this: *<BLINK>This is blinking text</BLINK>*. Don't use it. Rather than draw attention to your auction, it makes it harder to read and tacky-looking.

Take a close look at the text, examining the tags to see how you think the text will display. The next figure shows what the page looks like in a browser.

Easy, wasn't it? Now that you know the basics of handling text, we'll move on to fonts.

Changing and Colorizing Fonts

When you create an HTML page, the text that appears will be standard, black Times Roman by default. You can make your auction listing more unique by changing the font, the font size, and the color of the text and font.

To change the font, use the following command:

<FONT FACE="fontname">text goes here</FONT>

where **fontname** is the name of a font you want to use. If you were going to use the Helvetica font, the command would be

<FONT FACE="Helvetica">text goes here</FONT>

Keep in mind that you should use only common fonts that are found on most people's computers. In other words, try to stay with the normal fonts that came on your computer, and stay away from extra fonts you've bought or that came with other programs. Arial and Helvetica, in addition to Times Roman, are always good bets.

Changing the Size of the Font

You can also control the size of the text as well. You can make it larger or smaller than the default text that displays on a Web page. As with a headline, you don't specify an exact size for the text. Instead, you specify a relative size, from –6 (the smallest) to 6 (the biggest). To change the size of the text, use the following command:

<FONT SIZE="-2">text goes here</FONT>

This code will display the Times Roman text in a small text size. The following figure shows you the range of sizes available to you in Times Roman.

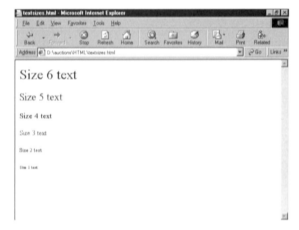

Here's the range of sizes you can display using the default Times Roman font.

You can combine changing the font with changing the font size to display a variety of fonts in different sizes. If you wanted to display the largest sized text available (size 6) in Helvetica, you'd use the following command:

<FONT FACE="Helvetica" size=6>text goes here</FONT>

Keep in mind that there's no real reason, in auction listings, to use very small fonts. You want everything clear and readable, and using fonts that are too small will only frustrate potential bidders.

Changing the Color of Text

To really jazz up your auction page, you can use colored text. You can add color to headlines or to body text. In fact, you can add

How to draw horizontal lines

Horizontal lines can be used to set off a title or to separate different sections of the listing. To draw a horizontal line use the *<HR>* tag and a line will be drawn at that spot across the page.

color to any text on the page. The following command for changes the color of text:

<FONT COLOR= "#colorcode">text goes here</FONT>

where **colorcode** is a combination of six letters and numbers that specifies a specific color. The code for blue is 0000FF, so the following command would make text blue:

<FONT COLOR="#0000FF">text goes here</FONT>

The following is a list of the most commonly used color codes:

Color	Code
Blue	0000FF
Black	000000
Brown	A52A2
Cyan	00FFFF
Dark Blue	00008B
Dark Gray	A9A9A9
Dark Green	006400
Gold	FFD700
Gray	808080
Green	00FF00
Magenta	FF00FF
Red	FF0000
Yellow	FFF00
White	FFFFFF

The color code can be combined with other font codes. For example, if you wanted to have green, bold Helvetica text displayed in size 5, you'd use the following command:

<FONT FACE="Helvetica" SIZE="5"
COLOR="#00FF00"><B>Text goes here:</B></FONT>

Beware of the "ransom note" effect

Don't be tempted to change fonts, text sizes, and text colors willy-nilly on your auction page. When you mix too many on a single page, it gets difficult to read and will chase bidders away.

Other Useful HTML Commands for Creating Auctions

There are a number of other useful HTML tags you can use to make your auctions as eye-catching and as useful as possible. You can use HTML to create bulleted lists, link to other pages, and display pictures. I won't cover in detail how to use pictures in this chapter. For that, turn to Chapter 15, "A Picture's Worth a Bigger Bid."

How to Create Bulleted and Numbered Lists

A particularly effective way to list the features and information about an item you have for sale is with lists. With lists of this kind, it's easy for potential buyers to quickly scan everything they need to know about what you have for sale.

You can use HTML to create bulleted lists and numbered lists. To create a bulleted list, you use the *<UL>* and *</UL>* tags around the list, and then use the *<LI>* code for each item on the list, as shown in the following:

<UL>

<LI>First item

  <LI>Second item

    <LI>Third item

  <LI>Fourth item

</UL>

You'll notice that I indented the code for each item the list. That indentation isn't actually needed—the browser ignores indentations like that. I put in the indent only so that it's easy for me to scan my own HTML after I create it. This way, it's easy for me to see where I've created a list. I suggest that you do the same, although it's not necessary for the HTML tags to work.

You create a numbered list almost identically, except that the commands you use around the list are *<OL>* and *</OL>*. The following code creates a numbered list:

<OL>

<LI>First item

  <LI>Second item

    <LI>Third item

  <LI>Fourth item

</OL>

The following figures shows examples of both bulleted and numbered lists.

*Here's how bul-
leted and num-
bered lists look in
a browser.*

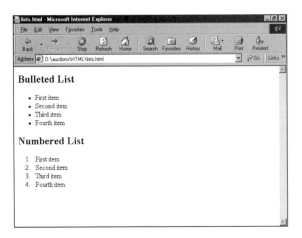

How to Link to Other Web Pages

HTML allows you to link to other pages, so someone can click a link in a page and immediately go to another Web page. This ability to link to other Web pages is an extremely useful HTML feature for auctioneers. You can use it to link to all of your other auctions, increasing visibility for them all. If you have a business on the Web where you sell items similar to the one you're selling at the auction, you can link to that as well. You also can link to pages that offer more information about the item you have for sale. In fact, the ways you can use this feature are boundless.

You'll use the following code for linking to other pages:

<A HREF="URL">Here's a link</A>

where **URL** is the location of the Web page to which you're linking.

Let's say that you're linking from the auction page to a home page you've created on your Internet Service Provider's (ISP) Web site. The location of your page there is *http://www.myisp.net/users/mypage.html.* Issue the following command:

<A HREF="http://www.myisp.net/users/mypage.html">Click here to get to my home page</A>

When you do this, only the "Click here to get to my home page" actually shows up on the Web page. It shows up as an underlined link, the same as any other. By the way, keep in mind that you have to include the *http://* in the address when using the linking command.

Put a *mailto* link on your auction page

The easier it is for potential bidders to get in touch with you, the more likely they'll contact you, and the more likely it is that they'll bid on what you're selling. So it's a good idea to put a *mailto* link on your Web page—a link that when clicked will launch the user's email program and create a new email message already addressed to you. While it's true that auction sites generally have your email address on them, that address is often separated from the item description itself, so people might not be likely to click it. They'll be more likely to send you email directly from the item description.

You create a *mailto* link in the same way you create a link to a Web page. The command is

<A HREF="mailto:youremailaddress">Click this link to send me email</A>

So if your email address was *preston@gralla.com*, the *mailto* command would be

<A HREF="mailto:preston@gralla.com">Click this link to send me email</A>

How to Use Pictures in Your Auction Listing

One of the most effective ways to make use of your auction listing is to include a picture of an item in it. I won't go into too much detail about pictures in this chapter—for that, turn to Chapter 15.

To link to a picture, use the following command:

<IMG SRC="URL">

where **URL** is the location and name of your graphic. Note that you don't need to use an end tag for the graphic command.

For example, if your picture was named *mypicture.jpg*, and was located on the *http://www.myisp.net/users/* directory and server, the command would be

<IMG SRC="http://www.myisp.net/users/mypicture.jpg">

As you'll see in the next chapter, pictures have to be in one of several special graphics formats to be included on a Web page.

How to Include the HTML Code on Your Auction Pages

So far in this chapter, you've learned how to use HTML to create code for better-looking and more effective Web pages. But how do you actually include that code on your auction listing? On most sites, such as eBay, you fill out a form to create an auction listing. After that form is filled out, the auction site automatically creates your listing, which is, in fact, an HTML page. So how to get your special coding in there?

How you do this varies from site to site, so it's best to check the individual site that you're using. On eBay, you paste the code into the Description area of the form you use to create an auction, shown in the following figure.

Here's how to include HTML in your auction listing on eBay.

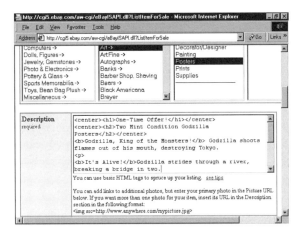

You create your HTML in Notepad or some other program, copy all the HTML to the clipboard, and then paste it from the clipboard into the form on eBay.

There are a few important things to keep in mind when using HTML on eBay:

- *You can't use HTML in your auction title*—It will interfere with eBay's search function, and then people won't find your item when searching. Additionally, the HTML commands won't be recognized and displayed.

- *You shouldn't use quotation marks in your HTML—*
  Throughout this chapter, I've included quotation marks in
  many HTML commands, because that's the way HTML is
  traditionally done. On eBay, however, those quotation marks
  can cause problems, so don't use them. Don't worry, it won't
  affect your HTML.

- *Review your HTML before and after posting it—*Nothing will
  make you look worse than presenting a sloppy-looking auction listing with odd-looking commands, characters, and
  spaces showing. Review your HTML before pasting it into
  the auction listing, and then review the final listing carefully
  before posting it. It's easy to make tiny errors in HTML that
  have big consequences when your page is posted.

Other Software for Creating HTML Pages

Until now, I've recommended that you use Notepad for creating
your HTML pages. It's simple, quick, and easy, and using it will
give you a familiarity with HTML.

But there are also many programs that will create HTML for you,
without you having to know much HTML. The following are just
a few of them:

- *Microsoft FrontPage Express—*FrontPage Express is a free
  HTML editor that Microsoft includes as part of Microsoft
  Internet Explorer and as a free download. You can create
  HTML pages without having to know HTML code—a set of
  tools lets you change fonts and text sizes, add pictures and
  links, and similar features.

- *Netscape Composer—*This one comes for free as part of
  Netscape Communicator. As with FrontPage Express, you'll
  be able to create HTML pages without having to know
  HTML code.

- *HomeSite—*This exceedingly powerful HTML editor is used
  by many Web professionals. It has more features and power
  than you'd ever need, but if you ever decide you want to get
  serious about HTML, this is the one to get. You can get a free
  evaluation copy of the program at *www.allaire.com*. If you

**For More
Information**

Many auction sites,
such as eBay and
Amazon, include
message boards that
include advice about
how to handle HTML
and pictures. On
eBay, for example,
click Community,
and then click the
Images/HTML Board
link.

want to use it after the evaluation period, you'll have to pay for it.

Keep in mind that no matter what HTML editor you use, you'll have to cut and paste the final HTML code into your auction listing.

Using Software for Designing Auctions

Some software has been created specifically for designing HTML-based auction pages. This kind of software will create entire auction listings for you, and many of them include templates that already include complete designs. All you need to do is put in your information, and you'll get a complete auction listing. The following lists some of the most popular software for this:

- *AuctionAssistant*—In addition to creating HTML auctions for you, AuctionAssistant also helps you track your auctions. You can get a free evaluation copy from *http://www. blackthornesw.com*; if you want to keep it, you'll have to pay $59.95.

- *Virtual Auction Ad Pro*—This software creates HTML auctions for you. An evaluation copy is available for free. If you want to keep it, you'll have to pay $15.95. Get it at *http://www.ungo.net/Software/Auction/vaap.htm*.

- *The Auction Secretary*—Like the others, The Auction Secretary creates HTML auctions for you. It costs $39.95. Get it at *http://www.the-store.com/auction2.html*.

There's also a Web site, *www.auctiondesigner.com*, that lets you create auction pages directly from it and includes predesigned templates for creating auctions. The site also hosts graphics files for you to use at your auctions. There are several levels of service; the least expensive starts at $7.95 per month.

For More Information

If you want to learn more about HTML, check out three excellent books: *Sams Teach Yourself HTML in 24 Hours*, *Sams Teach Yourself HTML 4.0 in 10 Minutes*, and *Sams Teach Yourself to Create Web Pages in 24 Hours*.

Going, Going, Gone!

One of the best ways to dress up your listings so that they draw more buyers is to use HTML, the language of the Web. HTML lets you add different fonts, colors, pictures, headlines, links, and many other things that will help your auction sell. The following is what auctioneers need to know about HTML:

- HTML pages are text pages that contain special commands that browsers interpret to display text, graphics, and links.

- HTML tags are enclosed within brackets. Many tags require a *start tag* and an *end tag*. The start tag issues a command, and the end tag turns the command off. So to make text bold, you would issue the command *<B>This is boldfaced text</B>*, and the text between the tags would be bold.

- HTML lets you create six levels of headlines, with *<H1>* being the largest and *<H6>* being the smallest.

- Other HTML commands allows you to center text, italicize text, specify a particular font, specify a font size, change the color of any text, create bulleted and numbered lists, and link to other Web pages.

- You can get special software, called HTML editors, that will help you build Web pages. You can also buy auction-building software that will build HTML-based auction pages. The auction-building software often includes templates that are pre-designed auction pages.

- After you create your HTML code, paste it into the form you use to create an auction listing on an auction site. Make sure to read the instructions on your auction site carefully—some auction sites have special requirements when it comes to using HTML.

CHAPTER 15

A Picture's Worth a Bigger Bid

Here's one of the simplest rules about auctions you'll ever come across: Pictures sell. When you include a picture in your auction, it has a greater chance of selling—and for more money—than if no picture is included. In short, when it comes to auctions, pictures are worth more than a thousand words—they're worth money as well.

In this chapter, you'll learn how you can increase auction sales by adding pictures to your listing. You'll discover where to get pictures, how to prepare them for posting, how you'll store them before they can be posted, and how you can include them in your auction listing.

Step One: How to Get a Picture in the Right Format

If you want pictures in your auction listing, the first thing you'll need to do is get the pictures from somewhere. As I'll teach you in this section, there are a lot of different ways for you to get pictures to spice up your auction listing.

Before teaching you how to get the pictures, though, you'll first need to know what format they need to be in. On the Web pictures generally should be in one of two different formats: GIF (which stands for Graphical Interchange Format) and JPEG (which stands for Joint Picture Experts Group). Files in the GIF format end in a .gif extension, and files in the JPEG format end in a .jpg extension. Graphics programs and other software give you a choice of formats to save in, and just about all of them will let you save files in either of these formats.

What You'll Learn in This Chapter

► How to acquire a picture and make sure it's in the right format.

► How to adjust a picture so that it will look the best in your auction listing.

► How to upload the picture to a Web server so that it can be used in your auction listing.

► How to include the picture in your auction listing.

Both formats compress graphics so they aren't too large to be easily displayed on the Web. If graphics are large, they take a long time to download, and then Web surfing slows to a crawl. Either format will work fine for your graphics, but if you want your graphics to provide the maximum impact, you should know the following about each:

- JPEG does a better job of compressing photographs and art with fine detail and gradations, so choose it if you'll be putting a photograph or detailed image on your auction page. It doesn't do as well with high-contrast images, such as line art.

- GIF works best for line art, cartoons, and similar graphics, so choose it for these types of pictures. It's not as good as JPEG for displaying photographs.

Where to Get Pictures for Your Auction

Now that you understand graphics formats, it's time to find the places where you can get pictures for your auction. It's quite easy to get pictures these days. The following are all the ways you can do it:

- *Take a photograph using a digital camera*—Digital cameras are an excellent way to get pictures into your computer. They store pictures on their own hard disk. After you take the pictures, you transfer them to your computer. You'll be able to save them in a Web-friendly graphics format as outlined earlier (GIF or JPEG).

Tip:
If you have a NetCam, such as 3COM's HomeConnect camera or Logitech's QuickCam, you can use them like digital cameras to take pictures. Check the documentation for how to do it.

- *Take a photograph with a regular camera and put it into your computer with a scanner*—You can buy a good quality scanner for under $200. They'll do a good job of converting a normal photograph into an image of a high-enough quality that you can put it on your Web site.

- *Take a photograph with a regular camera and ask that the photo lab convert the pictures to a computer format and give them to you on a disk, CD-ROM, or over the Web*—Pretty much any self-respecting photo service will do this for you these days. It's an easy way to get auction pictures without having to spend any money for hardware.

Try America Online's "You've Got Pictures" feature

If you're an America Online user, it's exceptionally easy to get pictures into your computer from a regular camera. Take your pictures as you normally would, and then take the film into a photo developer that participates in the "You've Got Pictures" plan. (There shouldn't be a problem finding one because there are over 38,000 developers that participate.)

When you fill out your envelope for developing the film, check the America Online box and put in your screen name. Pick up your photos as you normally would—they'll be normal photos. Then, within 48 hours, the photos will be delivered to your America Online account. When you log in, you'll hear the familiar America Online voice telling you, "You've got pictures!" Use the keyword Pictures, and you'll go to an area that will have an album of all your pictures. Follow the directions for saving them to your computer. When saving the pictures, make sure to save them in the *.jpg* format because that's the format you'll use for posting them on your auction listing.

- *Take a photograph with a regular camera and take the print to a printing or scanning service*—Many printing services, such as Kinko's, will scan in photographs and give them to you in any format you want. It's a cheap and easy way to get pictures into your computer without having to buy hardware. Unlike with photo services, you can have single photos scanned this way—you won't have to pay for putting the whole roll of film onto disk.

Getting Pictures from the Web

Another excellent place to get pictures to put in your auction are from the Web itself. The Web is full of pictures of all kinds—and what makes these pictures especially useful for you is that they're already in the proper format you need for posting online. Another bonus is that not only are they in the proper format, often the pictures have been tweaked and manipulated so that they'll look best online.

There are many different sources for pictures on the Web. One of the best places I've found is the Pictures and Sounds section of the Lycos site. To get there, go to *www.lycos.com* and click the

Pictures link. You'll then be able to search for pictures among the many thousands available on the Internet.

Another way to find pictures of an item you're selling is to go the manufacturer's Web site. Many will include pictures of their products right on the Web page. Many online shopping sites, such as *www.buy.com*, also include pictures of products. If you find a picture on a Web page, it's easy to download and save it to your computer. Just follow these steps:

1. Right-click the picture you want to save.

2. From the menu that appears, choose Save Picture As or Save Image As, depending on which browser you use. The following figure shows you the process of saving a picture of a 3Com HomeConnect digital Web camera.

3. Choose the directory where you want to save the image. It's that simple.

Here's how you can copy any image you find on a Web page to your own PC.

Be careful not to violate copyright laws

When you copy a picture from a Web page onto your computer, you have to make sure that you're not violating any copyrights. Sometimes pictures posted on the Web carry copyrights. Check the Web site to see if the images posted are copyrighted or not.

Step Two: Prepare Your Picture to Be Put Online

As you learned earlier in the chapter, the pictures you post on the Web need to be in a special format. But often, just making sure the pictures are in the right format isn't enough. You also want to make sure that they'll have maximum impact. To do that, you'll need to use a graphics program. If you have a scanner or digital camera, a graphics program probably came with it. Graphics programs often come with many computers as well.

If you don't have a graphics program, try out Paint Shop Pro. You can get it from the *www.jasc.com* Web site. You can download and try it for free for 30 days. If you like it, you'll need to pay for it at the end of the trial period. The following figure shows Paint Shop Pro at work.

Paint Shop Pro is an excellent program for dressing up graphics you want to put on your auction page.

You need to know the following about preparing your pictures before you post them on your auction:

- *Keep images small*—Large images slow down your auction page from displaying. The longer your auction page takes to display, the greater the chance that people won't stay around to bid because they'll become frustrated waiting for the page to load. You'll lose bidders. Try to keep the size of your image to 30KB or less.

- *Crop images so that they're as tight as possible on the item you're selling*—Cropping a picture means cutting out unnecessary parts of it so that it's small, loads quickly, and the person buying it can see it clearly without any distractions. Any graphics program will have cropping tools.

- *Adjust the brightness and contrast so that the image is as clear and bright as possible*—If your image is muddy, dull, and hard to see, buyers won't really know what it is they're

buying. Use your graphics program's contrast tools to
brighten and sharpen the image. Next is a picture of a poster
of Godzilla being sharpened and brightened with Paint Shop
Pro.

*Here's how to
adjust the bright-
ness and contrast
of an image with
Paint Shop Pro so
that it's as clear
and bright as pos-
sible for posting
to the Web.*

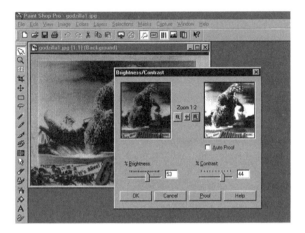

Make Sure Your Picture Isn't Too Large

When you take a digital photo or scan in an image, very often the
picture you end up with will have a very large file size. You
shouldn't post large files on an auction page. When you post a
large file, it takes a long time for the browser to load the page—
and many potential bidders won't wait for the page to load.
Instead, they'll bid elsewhere, and you'll lose a sale.

Because of this, you should shrink the size of your pictures before
posting them. Keep them to 20KB or less. You shrink their sizes
by compressing them. When you compress a picture, it's not as
sharp-looking, but you don't need to show super-high resolution
photos to make a sale—bidders just want to see a basic picture of
what it is they're bidding on.

Graphics programs, such as Paint Shop Pro, let you compress pictures in the JPEG format. The following steps show how to do it
in Paint Shop Pro:

1. Open the file you want to compress.

2. Choose Save As from the File menu.

3. In the screen that appears, click the Options button.

4. A new screen will appear, as pictured next. Use the slider at
   the bottom to choose the amount of compression. When you
   slide it to the right, you increase the compression, which
   shrinks the file size but also will decrease image quality.

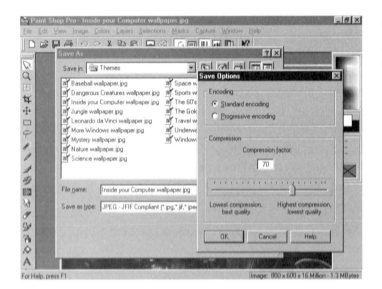

*Here's how you'll
compress the size
of JPEG files using
Paint Shop Pro.*

5. Choose the compression ratio you want and save the file.
   When you save the file, save it under a new name, leaving
   your original file intact. That way, you can save the file several times, testing different compression ratios to see which
   offers the smallest file size while still maintaining a reasonable image quality.

Step Three: Store Your Picture on a Web Server

After you've prepared your picture to be put in your auction,
you'll need to store it in on a Web server somewhere on the
Internet. It's not good enough to simply have the picture on your
own computer. When it's only on your computer, it won't be
available to people who browse the Internet. Instead, it needs to
be on a Web server that includes special software for making pictures available. Then, after it's on the server, you'll be able to link

to the picture using HTML commands that I'll teach you later in this chapter.

There's a two-step process for storing your pictures on a Web server. First, you need to find a Web server where you can store the pictures. Then you'll need to upload the pictures to the server. I'll cover both of those steps in the rest of this section.

Where to Find Free Web Servers for Storing Pictures

Auction sites include powerful Web servers, so you might think that they'd be ideal places to store your pictures. Well, they are perfect places, but most auction sites, such as eBay and Amazon, won't allow you to store your pictures there. Their servers would get so full of pictures that they'd have a hard time doing anything else, such as delivering auction information. You're going to have to find other places for storing your pictures on the Web. You can get free storage space at the following places:

- *The first place to check is with your Internet Service Provider (ISP)*—Many ISPs offer you storage space for free—often of 10MB or more—where you can host a Web site. Even if you don't host your own Web site, you can still use that storage space for anything you want, including storing pictures. My ISP, the Internet Access Company (TIAC), offers 10MB of storage space, and so that's one place where I put auction pictures.

- *If you use America Online, you get free storage space*— America Online lets you create your own home page for free, and you can store pictures in the same place on a Web server where you have a home page. For information about your home page an storage space, use the keywords HOME PAGE.

- *Many Internet sites will let you create home pages and get storage space for free*—There are many places on the Internet that let you create home pages for free. Among the most popular are *www.geocities.com*, *www.tripod.com*, *www.xoom.com*, *www.theglobe.com*, and *www.angelfire.com*.

America Online even has a site on the Internet where non-America Online members can create home pages for free at *www.hometown.aol.com*, shown in the following figure. On all these sites, you'll be able to store your pictures in the same place where you store your home pages.

Among the many places where you can store auction pictures is the AOL Hometown site at www.hometown.aol.com.

- *The www.auctionwatch.com and www.auctionrover.com sites will store auction pictures for you for free*—The sites also have a great deal of useful information and news about auctions, so you'll want to visit them for other reasons as well.

How to Send Your Picture to a Web Server

Once you have a picture, and you've chosen which Web server you're going to use for storage, its time to send your picture to the server. The term commonly used for sending your picture to a server is to *upload* it.

The way you'll upload your picture to a server depends on the server to which you're uploading. Many the Internet sites that let you create free Web pages, such as GeoCities, include tools and file managers built right into them for uploading files and pictures. So does *www.auctionwatch.com*. To upload pictures with most of these tools, you'll only need to know the directory where you stored the pictures on your computer.

You'll have to do more than store pictures on Web page-creation sites like GeoCities

Sites like GeoCities generally require that you create your own home page on them, not merely use them as storage space for your auction pictures. If you don't create a home page there, they can kick you off and take away your storage privileges.

If you're uploading your picture to your own ISP and to certain Web sites, however, you'll have to use a special program called an FTP program. There are many you can use, but my favorite is called WS FTP. You can try it out for free by downloading it from many Internet download sites including ZDNet Downloads at *www.hotfiles.com*. The following picture shows how you'll upload a file using the program.

Here's how you'll upload a picture to your ISP using the popular FTP program called WS FTP.

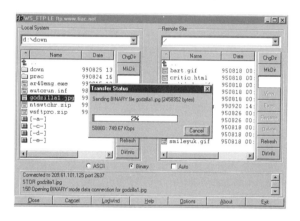

When you upload files, they still stay on your computer

When you upload a file, that file still stays on your computer—it won't vanish. You're only uploading a copy of your file; the original stays on your hard drive.

No matter how you upload the picture, you have to copy the exact location and filename of where you've sent it. If you're sending the file to your ISP, you'll have gotten the exact location to which you can upload from your ISP. You'll attach the filename to that. So, for example, if the location where you upload your file to is *http://www.tiac.net/users/bigguy/* and the filename is *godzilla1.jpg*, the location would be *http://www.tiac.net/users/bigguy/godzilla.jpg*.

The same holds true for using a free Web page service such as GeoCities. The upload manager that you use for those sites will tell you the location of the files when you upload them, so be sure to write down the location. As you'll see in the next section, you'll need that to put pictures in your auction.

Step Four: How to Include Your Pictures in Auction Listings

Now everything's set. You've gotten your pictures, massaged them so that they're the way you like them, and uploaded them to a

Web server. Now you're ready to include them in an auction listing.

Each site has different ways of including pictures in your auction. Generally, though, there are two different ways:

- Including pictures using built-in tools at the auction site

- Including pictures using HTML

I'll teach you how to do both in this section. As an example, we'll say that the picture we'll include is the *godzilla1.jpg* file that's stored at *http://www.tiac.net/users/pgralla/*, which means that the entire location is *http://www.tiac.net/users/pgralla/godzilla1.jpg*.

How to Include Pictures Using an Auction Site's Tools

Most auction sites include tools that let you include photos in your auction listing. The general way you'll do this is the same— you'll do it when creating your auction listing. In practice, they all work slightly differently. I'll show you how to use eBay to include a picture in a listing.

Create your auction listing as you normally do on eBay. Then, in the Picture URL field, include the exact location of your image, including the filename of the image. In the next figure, you can see that I've put in *http://www.tiac.net/users/pgralla/godzilla1.jpg*.

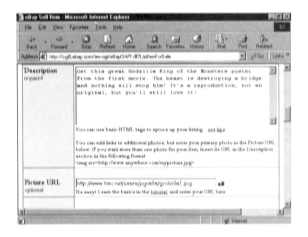

Here's the form you'll fill out to include a picture in your auction listing on eBay.

When you're done with the listing, click Review as you normally would. In the page that appears, scroll down until you get to the area titled Picture URL. You should see the URL of your picture and then the picture itself, as shown in the following figure.

You'll be able to see your picture in the review page of your eBay listing. If there's a broken link, go back and make sure the URL you put in is correct.

On other auction sites, you follow similar directions. On Amazon, for example, you include the exact location of your image, including the filename of the image. Then, when you click Preview Your Auction, you'll be able to preview what your auction will look like, including the picture, as shown in the following figure.

Here's how you'll preview how your picture will look on Amazon auctions.

If there's a broken link and no picture is showing up, that means you've made a mistake entering the URL. Go back and check it, and then put in the correct URL.

How to Include Pictures Using HTML

When you use an auction site's tools for putting pictures on your auction listing, you have no real control over where that listing goes. It goes to the default location chosen by the Web site. On eBay, for example, the picture goes after the description and before the bidding information.

You can use HTML instead to place pictures in your auction listing. This way, you'll have control over where the picture goes. On eBay, for example, you'll be able to include a picture in the description itself, so you can mix a picture in with the description.

You place pictures in HTML using the same HTML conventions that you learned in the previous chapter. To place a picture using HTML, use the following code:

<IMG SRC=URL>

where *URL* is the actual location URL of your picture.

Note that you need to include the *http://* portion of the URL. For our example, the code for putting in a graphic would be

<IMG SRChttp://www.tiac.net/users/pgralla/godzilla1.jpg>

Going, Going, Gone!

Adding pictures to your auction listing is a great way to increase sales. The following lists what to know about how to add pictures to your auctions:

- To post your pictures to an auction listing, they'll have to be in the GIF or JPG file format. JPG works best for photographs and art with fine gradations, while GIF works best for line art and art that has high contrast.

- There are many ways you can get pictures to put in your auction listing. You can take a picture with a digital camera and transfer it to your computer, or you can take a picture with a normal camera and scan in the print. If you don't have a scanner, photo services will turn your negatives into computer files, or printing services will scan in photos for you.

- Visit the sites of manufacturers of products for pictures of items you're selling—you can download them to your computer and use them in auctions. Be sure to check copyright information about the pictures before downloading them.

- Prepare your pictures for posting by making sure they're not over 30KB in size, that they're bright and have good contrast, and that they're a closeup of the item you're selling.

- You'll need to store your pictures on a Web serve before they can be included in your auction listing. Your Internet Service Provider may have a free storage area for you. America Online and Web-page creation sites, such as *www.geocities.com*, include free storage.

- Include pictures in your auction listing by using the built-in tools on the auction site or by using the HTML command *<IMG SRC="URL">* where *URL* is the location and filename of your picture.

CHAPTER 16

Secret Tips for Creating Auctions That Sell

By now, you know how to create basic auctions. You've learned how to write effective auction copy, use HTML to dress up your auction, and how to add pictures to add pizzazz.

So far, so good. But there's still more that you can do to create auctions that sell. In this chapter we'll look at tips to help you increase your auction sales—such as finding items to offer, figuring out the right time to post and end your auctions, and publicizing your auctions to bring in more bidders.

Finding Good Stuff to Sell

Often, you'll already know what you want to sell before it even occurs to you that an online auction would be a good place to sell it—that elephant cookie jar in the garage has been screaming "sell me" for years.

But if you're looking to pick up cash beyond the value of your white elephants, you may need to scrounge for some wares to put online. Here are a few suggested sources for acquiring auctionables.

Buy at School and Church "White Elephant" Sales

Many schools and churches hold annual fund-raisers of different kinds. Often, one of the most popular parts of the fund raiser are "white elephant" sales—sales in which parents of children at the school or people at a church donate items to be sold. These white elephant sales often turn up items of a surprisingly high quality. Clothing, books, and toys are often popular sale items, and, in recent years, software has become popular as well. The prices you'll pay for the items is often exceedingly low. It's a chance to find some truly great deals.

Check Out Garage, Yard, Block, and "Tag" Sales

During the spring and the fall, you'll find many garage, yard, and "tag" sales (tag sales are just another word for garage and yard sales). At these sales, people clean out their garages and houses and sell what they no longer want. They're great places to find treasures of all kinds—toys, albums, clothing, and many other kinds of goods. Your selection at the end, of course, won't be that substantial, but you'll get great prices or sometimes pay nothing.

Sometimes several houses or an entire neighborhood band together to hold block sales, and there you'll have the greatest number of items from which to choose.

Sometimes garage, yard, block, and tag sales are advertised in the newspaper. More often, they're advertised via word of mouth and flyers taped to telephone poles and pinned to neighborhood bulletin boards, such as those at a supermarket. Check those places regularly to see if any sales are happening.

Buy from College Students in the Spring

Every spring, in university towns across America, there's a vast migration as students leave college to go back home or on vacation for the summer. That means there's a huge number of goods available for sale, and often quite inexpensively.

Check areas near universities around the time that students leave, and look on college bulletin boards at that time of year for notices of sales as well.

Buy Items to Sell at Auction Sites

Auction sites are good places to do research to find out if things you have laying around the house might be worth selling. But they're good for another reason for sellers: You can buy items at auction sites with the express purpose of going out and selling them. In other words, you can haunt auction sites in the same way that you do flea markets, looking for bargains that you know you can sell at a profit.

Early birds get the goods

There's one thing to keep in mind at school and church sales: Come early, as soon as the sale opens. Even an hour after the sale opens, the best items are often gone.

Latecomers pick up bargains

At garage sales, early birds get the best selection. But if you come near the end of the sale, prices may drop, and you can pick up the leftovers cheap—or even free!

You'll have to be careful and do your homework if you want to buy items this way. After all, the item has been out in the open and up for bid once, and no one has bid high on it. You'll have to be pretty sure that you're getting a great deal to buy it— otherwise, you'll be forced to sell at a loss.

Check auctions to see what's popular

You'd be amazed at the things that sell at auctions. At times, it seems like anything that's ever been created or manufactured has become a collectible. Old vinyl records, old license plates, jars, clothing you uncover during spring cleaning, costume jewelry—there's no end to the number of odd things that collectors will bid on and buy at auctions.

But how do you know what's junk, and what might be worth collecting? Spend time on the auction sites, especially eBay because it's the largest auction site there is. Spend a good amount of time browsing through the listings. There are thousands of them, so it'll take you some time, but it'll be worth it. See what's selling on auction sites, and then if you have it laying around the house, put it up for auction. Even if it doesn't sell, you won't have lost much money—often well under a dollar for most items.

When you find something laying around your house or attic, go online and see if anything similar to it is being sold. If it is, you may have a treasure on your hands.

Buy at Estate Sales

Estate sales are excellent places for finding collectibles to sell at online auctions. Estate sales advertise in the newspapers, so make a habit of checking the newspaper for them.

Depending on how long the sale lasts, you may or may not be able to buy items discounted. You may be able to get discounts a day or two after the opening.

Sign in, please...

Arrive at estate sales a few hours before they start; sometimes, you must sign your name to a list in advance, to get in.

Go to Flea Markets and Swap Meets

Flea markets and swap meets are great places to find collectibles and items of all kinds to sell at auctions. They're generally advertised in newspapers, so check your local papers for them. Many flea markets are held on a regularly scheduled basis, weekly, monthly, biannually or annually, so find out the schedules for each.

As with other kinds of sales, it's best to get there as early as possible; often, the best deals are gone within a few hours of the flea market opening. At flea markets, you'll find sellers who are regulars and may make their living that way, as well as one-time sellers. One-time sellers may have the best deals because they often don't know the value of what they have for sale. On the other hand, they often have the most junk as well.

If you find a regular at a flea market who often has goods you're interested in buying, get a business card or contact information from him. That way, you can get in touch without having to go to the flea market, and may get his best items.

Try Bric-a-Brac Stores

In many neighborhoods, you'll find bric-a-brac stores—stores that are just one step above a yard sale and are filled with a variety of different used items for sale. Depending on the store and its location, they can be excellent places to find items to sell at online auctions.

In general, if you find a store like this in an expensive neighborhood, it'll bill itself as an antique store (no matter what's for sale inside), and you'll pay top-dollar for the goods. It'll be tough for you to make a profit if you then resell the item. In less-expensive neighborhoods, these stores can be good places to pick up bargains.

Read the Classified Ads

If you're going to get serious about finding things to sell at auctions, read your local newspaper's classified ad section every day. Anything you might want to buy, you'll find for sale there. Classified ads are also a good place to find out about flea markets and other similar kinds of places where you can buy inexpensive collectibles and goods.

Check Your Garage, Basement, and Attic

Finally, often the best place to find items for sale are closest to home—your own house. Many people squirrel away all kinds of goods for storage at home—clothing, old records, and a huge variety of miscellany. These goods may sit unused for a decade or more—and very often, odd old goods are the very things that collectors are looking for most.

Take an inventory of all the things you have in storage that you really don't need any more, and then put those items up for auction. You may be surprised at how much you'll find to sell.

Start and End Your Auctions at the Right Time for Maximum Impact

Here's one of the most important secrets you should know about auctions: The time that you begin and end your auctions can make a big effect on whether you have bidders and how high they bid.

Why is that? Why should one time be any better than another? It's because of the existence of auction "snipers" and those who like to bid close to the end of the auction to get the best possible deal. Many bidders haunt auction sites, checking what auctions are in the process of closing, or are near closing, and then they bid.

So what does this have to do with when your auctions begin and end? You want your auctions to end at the time when you have the greatest possible audience. If your auction ends at a time when there's the greatest audience, the most people possible will notice your auction's closing, so you'll have the most bidders.

The U.S. spans four time zones, so you want to pick a time for your auction to end when the maximum number of people are likely to be logged on to the Internet at an auction site. It should be after work hours—most people don't spend a lot of time bidding on auctions during work (or at least they shouldn't, if they want to keep their jobs). Your auction should end enough after work for people to come home and get online. Given that, you'd want your auction to end sometime after 6:30 PST, which is 9:30 EST. It shouldn't end too late on the East Coast, or you'll lose a lot of bidders.

eBay's clock is set to West Coast time

The eBay clock, which shows the current time on the site and time-stamps auctions, is set to Pacific Standard Time (PST).

Based on all this, your auction is best ending sometime between 6:30 and 8:30 PST—that's the time when you'll get the greatest number of active bidders.

Knowing when your auction should end will determine when it should begin. Auctions end a set number of days after you create your listing—for example, three, five, or seven days (your choices on eBay). They end at the exact time that you created them. So make sure to create your auctions at the time you want them to end.

All this applies if you're ending your auction on a weekday. But if you're ending it on a weekend, the time should be slightly different. In the next section, I'll teach you what you need to know about which day of the week you should start or end your auction and the time of day it should start and end.

Deciding Which Day of the Week Your Auction Should End

Now you have a good sense of the best time to start and end your auctions. But how about the day of the week?

No great surprise here: Weekends are good. Consider either starting or ending your auctions on a weekend, when people have more free time than they do on weekdays. If you do, adjust the starting and ending time accordingly. If you're starting or ending on a Saturday, don't do it during the evening when people may be out for dinner or entertainment. I'd suggest early afternoon EST. That way, you'll get East Coasters before they go out for the evening, and you'll still get West Coasters during the early afternoon.

Sunday late afternoons or evenings are good times, and I'd suggest doing it earlier than you do during workdays. Often on Sunday nights, people want to get to bed earlier than during the rest of the week to be rested before the week starts. From about 3 to 7 p.m. PST would be a good bet.

Deciding on the Best Time of Year for Auctions

Here's something that may surprise you: Certain times of the year are better than others for selling at auctions. Surprisingly, auction sites report that January is often one of the most active times for auctioning. It's not just that a good portion of the country is wrapped in winter. Many people also auction off gifts they received for the holidays that they really didn't want. This may sound as if it's a bad time to auction goods because there's so much competition. In fact, visitors to auction sites have learned that there's a lot of goods for sale in January, so there's a lot more bidders as well as sellers.

The other winter months are good times for auctions as well, because so many people are indoors. Spring tends to be a downtime, not only because the weather is getting better, but because in the early spring, at least, people are distracted by their taxes and the Internal Revenue Service. Summer is a mixed time—the weather is good and so people are less likely to be indoors. Starting in September, though, bidding picks up, and gets especially heavy throughout November and December as people shop for holiday gifts.

Of course, if you have something you want to sell and you don't want it laying around your garage or attic, you want to sell it whenever you can—just to get rid of it. Only follow this advice about when to sell if you have the luxury of selling only when you'll have the largest number of bidders.

Don't end your auctions on a holiday

Don't end your auctions on a holiday. That's when people often travel or spend time with their families, and are less likely to visit auction sites.

Deciding How Long an Auction Should Last

After you've decided when to end your auction and the day and time of year you want to hold it, it's time to figure how long your auction should last.

Different auction sites let you choose different lengths of time that your auction can last. On eBay, as well as on several other auction sites, you can choose three, five, or seven days. The following is what to you should know about each auction length:

- I'm a big fan of the seven-day auction. It exposes your auction for the longest length of time to the greatest number of potential bidders. If you choose a seven-day auction, you'll be assured that it's visible during the weekend no matter when you start it.

- On the other hand, I don't see much point to the five-day auction. If you need some quick cash and can't wait the two extra days for a seven-day auction, it might be worth your while. Otherwise, I don't see the point.

- Three-day auctions can be used to create a sense of excitement and urgency that you can't get in seven-day auctions. A title that contains the words "Must sell! 3 DAYS!" or "Fast sale! 3 DAYS ONLY!" will go a long way toward drawing in bidders who smell a good deal in the making.

Publicize Your Auctions to Bring in the Most Bidders

There's a simple rule of math that applies to auctions: The more people who know about your auctions, the more people will bid on them, and the more money you'll get.

To get the most money for your auction, you need to do more than simply create and post an auction listing. You need to publicize it as well. That way, you'll draw as many people as possible to your auction. The following are some ways you can publicize your auction:

- *Post messages on related Internet newsgroups, telling them about your auction and putting direct links right into the message*—There are many different newsgroup discussion areas where collectors congregate, and auctioneers commonly post auctions they're holding. Look for newsgroups that start with *alt.collecting*, such as *alt.collecting.beanie-babies*, *alt.collecting.barbies*, *alt.collecting.stamps*, and many others. Pictured next is a post to the *alt.collecting.records* newsgroup. Both Internet Explorer and Netscape Navigator include software for reading newsgroups. You can also read newsgroups at the *www.deja.com* Web site. One note: Make sure that the newsgroups you're posting to allow you to post commercial messages.

- *If you have your own Web page, advertise your auction there and include a link directly to it*—It'll draw extra people in.

- *Post messages about your auction on America Online messsage boards*—America Online has very active message boards about collectibles of every kind. Post messages there about your auction, including links to it.

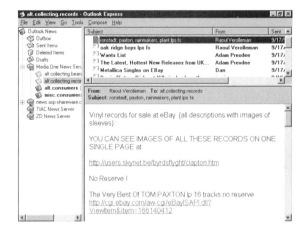

Let the world know about your auction by posting messages to related Internet newsgroups. Pictured here is someone posting a message about an auction of records taking place on eBay.

- *Post messages to Internet discussion areas, such as those found on Yahoo!*—Many Internet sites, such as *www.yahoo.com* and *www.excite.com*, include very active discussion areas about collectibles, buying and selling. Post messages there, including links to your auctions, as a way to draw more people to the bidding.

Other Tips for Increasing Your Auction Sales

There are other ways that you can increase your auction sales. Follow this advice and you'll have a better chance of selling your goods for top dollar:

- *Avoid setting reserve prices*—Many bidders don't like bidding on auctions that have reserve prices, so those auctions tend to draw fewer bidders. Unless you have a very good reason, don't set a reserve price.

- *Don't have multiple, simultaneous auctions in which you're selling similar items*—Have five Charizard Pokémon cards that you're looking to sell? Don't sell them in separate auctions all at once—you'll flood the market and bring down the price you get for each. Instead, hold auctions one at a time. You'll get the most money for your cards.

- *Re-list items that don't draw any bidders*—If no one buys what you have for sale, you'll spend very little money at an

Shop around for the best site

Before selling your item, check several auction sites and see which of them fetch the highest price for the item. Sell it there, not just at the site with which you're most familiar.

auction site—usually under a dollar. If something doesn't sell, create a new auction for it. Try changing the title and description and see what happens—you have little to lose.

Going, Going, Gone!

There's a big difference between creating an auction and creating an auction that sells. If you want to give your items the best chances of selling, you should know the following.

- Sell what you have on hand, but keep in mind that you can sell much more than merely your own unwanted stuff. Bargain sources such as school and church sales, garage sales, and flea markets all offer goods you may be able to buy cheap and then sell online at a profit.

- Have your auctions end at a time when the most number of potential buyers are likely to be looking at auctions that are about to close. A good time for them to end during the week is from about 6:30 to 8:30 p.m. Pacific Standard Time.

- It's often a good idea to end your auctions on weekends. If you end them on weekends, don't end them during a Saturday night. Sunday evenings or Saturday afternoons are a better time.

- January is a surprisingly busy time for auctions, so is a good month for selling things. So are all the winter months and the months from September through December.

- In general, a week is a good length of time for an auction to last. However, you can also create a sense of urgency for bidders if you set it at three days.

- Increase your auction sales by publicizing your auction on Internet newsgroups, America Online discussion areas, and discussion sites on the Internet.

PART 4

Completing the Deal

CHAPTER 17

Making Contact with the High Bidder

You've done your job well, and your item's been sold. Congratulations. It's time to enjoy the fruits of your labor. It's time to make contact with the high bidder and close the deal.

In this chapter, you'll learn all you need to know about getting in touch with the buyer, making sure all goes well, and getting your payment.

How You'll Be Notified About the High Bidder

After the auction closes, there are two ways to find out who the high bidder was. The first is to simply go to your auction listing. When the bidding is over, you'll get all the information you need there. The listing will tell you that the bidding is over and will include the high bid, as well as the username of the high bidder. This page will look different on different auction sites. On eBay, it looks like the following figure. As you can see, there's an "Auction has ended" notice next to the Time Left area, and all the relevant information about the auction is displayed.

When the auction closes, the links are all still live on this page. So, for example, if you want to send email to the high bidder, you can just click the link on the page.

This page is useful, but you may not remember every day to visit each auction listing you have, especially if you sell multiple items. An even better way to get notified that the auction has ended is with an email. When the auction ends, auction sites send emails out to both buyers and sellers giving all relevant information, including the final price, the time the auction ended, the number of bids, and the ID and email address of both the buyer

What You'll Learn in This Chapter

▶ The ways you can find out who the high bidder is.

▶ How to check feedback that others have given the high bidder.

▶ What you should tell the high bidder in the email you send shortly after the auction closes.

▶ The way that you'll complete the deal.

▶ How you can provide feedback to the auction site about the high bidder.

▶ How you'll pay the auction site for your auction.

and seller. The next figure is an example of the email that eBay sends out to sellers.

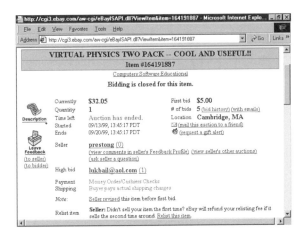

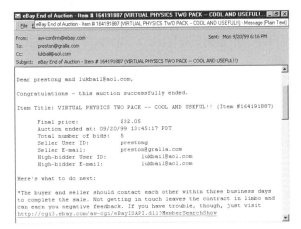

There's a lot of information contained in this email. The following is the rundown of the most important pieces of information in it. This refers to eBay, but other auction sites offer similar information:

- *Final price*—This is the final bid from the seller. It's what he'll be required to pay you.

- *Auction ended at*—The exact date and time the auction ended. Nice to know, but not really important for what you need to do next.

- *Total number of bids*—Useful information—the total number of bids tells you how hot and heavy the bidding was. This can help you determine how to price any similar items you have to sell in the future.

- *Seller User ID and Seller Email*—Your ID and email address. Make sure that both of these are accurate. If not, immediately get in touch with the auction site.

- *High-bidder User ID and High bidder Email*—The ID and email address of the high bidder. You'll use this information to get in contact with the high bidder, and you'll also use it to check out the high bidder's ratings.

When you get this piece of email, it means it's time to contact the high bidder. You should make contact as soon as possible. Some sites have rules about the amount of time within which you're supposed to make contact. On eBay, for example, you're supposed to make contact within three business days after the close of the auction.

Checking Out the Bidder's Feedback

Before making contact with the high bidder, you should first check out the bidder's feedback and history. This isn't strictly necessary, because you're under a contract to sell your item to the high bidder no matter what. But knowing the bidder's feedback will help you know how much slack to give the bidder if issues occur, such as late payments or similar problems.

The way you check the bidder's feedback varies from site to site. On eBay, as well as many other auction sites, first go back to the auction page where you sold your item. Look at the number next to the high bidder's ID—that will give you the total amount of net positive feedback about the bidder. To see a more comprehensive history, as well as all the feedback given by every individual about the bidder, click the number. You'll go to a page that shows every comment made by people about the buyer.

Again, you're required to sell to the high bidder, no matter what feedback you find. But in the event of late payments or other issues, you'll know to very quickly contact the second high bidder if the high bidder has negative feedback.

Completed auctions are visible for only 30 days

After an auction is completed, it doesn't stay live forever, either on eBay or other auction sites. After 30 days, the auction listing is taken down on eBay and will be no longer visible. If you need a copy of that auction page for some reason, copy it to your hard drive before the 30 days time period ends.

Contacting the High Bidder via Email

After you've checked out the high bidder's feedback rating, it's time to make contact. While you could wait for the high bidder to contact you, general etiquette is that the bidder waits for the seller to make contact. And because you're the one who wants to get an item off your hands and make a sale, it makes sense that you'd be the first to make contact.

You should be both friendly and business-like in you contact. Start off by thanking the bidder for making the high bid. Then include the following information in your note:

- *The name of the item he's made a high bid on*—To you, it may be obvious. But if the bidder has bid on numerous items, he'll need a reminder of what it is he's won.

- *A link to the auction page where he did the bidding*—That way he can get any information he wants from the site.

- *The total amount of money he should send to you*—Broken out to show both his high bid and the shipping costs.

- *The methods of payment you'll accept*—You've noted that on the auction page, but he may need to be reminded.

> **You can include a payment form via email for the buyer to fill out**
>
> To make sure that the buyer doesn't make any mistakes when paying, and to avoid misunderstandings, some sellers like to send a payment form to the high bidder via email when they make first contact with the bidder. The form can include the payment required, the name and address of the buyer and seller, the item being sold—all information pertinent to the sale. That way, you also have a paper record of the sale. The form can be sent as a Word document attached to the email message or can be part of the email message itself. The buyer will print it out and send it to you, along with his payment.

- *Your name and address*—So the buyer can send you the money.

- *Your email address*—So the buyer can get in touch with you if there are any questions or problems that arise.

- *A request for the bidder's name and mailing address*—So you can mail him the item after you receive payment and the payment clears.

How You Close the Deal

Shortly after you send the email to the high bidder, you should get an email in return. The buyer should acknowledge your message and give you his address so you can send him the item after receiving payment.

Now all you can do is wait. Within a few days of getting the email from the buyer, you should receive payment. If the payment is via money order or cashier's check, you can (and should) ship the item right away. If the payment is made via a personal check, wait for the check to clear before shipping the item.

In either case, as soon as you receive payment, notify the buyer that the payment has arrived. Tell the buyer when you plan to ship the item—if you've been paid via money order or cashier's check, tell him you're sending it out immediately. If you've been paid via personal check, tell the buyer you'll send the item as soon as the check clears.

For more details on accepting payment and on what to do if there are problems with being paid, turn to Chapter 18, "How To Accept Payment." And for information about shipping, turn to Chapter 19, "How To Ship Your Items."

Providing Buyer Feedback

After your end of the deal has been completed, you should provide feedback about the buyer. Auction sites can only work if people provide feedback about their experiences with others, so here's your chance to make sure that auction sites will continue to work and thrive.

The way you'll provide feedback varies from site to site, so check yours to see how to do it. On eBay, there will be a link in the email you were sent for providing feedback; simply follow that link and you'll go to a page, shown in the next figure, where you can provide feedback about the seller.

Here's how you
can provide
feedback on sell-
ers on eBay.

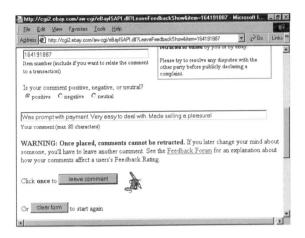

How You'll Pay the Auction Site

When the auction ends, you're not the only one who gets paid.
The auction site also requires payment—and you pay the auction
site, the bidder doesn't.

There are usually two fees associated with each auction you create: the fee you'll pay for listing an item and the fee you'll pay
after the auction is completed. The listing fee is based on the minimum bid or reserve price you've set for the item you're selling
plus any special placement fees, bold-faced listings, or similar
extra listing fees. The fee you'll pay for a completed auction is
based on the final selling price of the item. The fees vary from
site to site, so check yours to get information about fees.

**Even if no one bids
on your item, you
have to pay the auc-
tion site**

You'll have to pay
most auctions sites,
even if no one buys
what you have for
sale. The fee is low
and is based on the
minimum bid or
reserve price you set
for an item.

After the auction ends, you should check your account with your
auction site to see what you owe. Again, how you do this varies
from site to site. To check your account on eBay, click the
Services button on the main page, and from the page that appears,
click Check My Seller Account Status. After filling in your ID
and password, you'll go to a page similar to the one shown in the
next figure, which shows the status of your account. It gives you a
rundown of what you owe.

As you can see, I owe $1.68 for one of my completed auctions—
25 cents for a listing fee (what eBay calls an insertion fee), and
$1.43, based on the $32.05 selling price of my item.

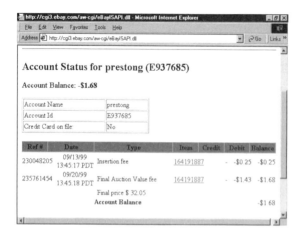

Time to pay the piper: Here's how to see how much you owe for selling your items on eBay.

Sites such as eBay give you several options for payment. You can give them your credit card number, and they'll automatically deduct the amount that's due every month. I find this the easiest way to pay the site—there's no chance that I'll forget to pay and so get assessed late fees, or even worse, have trading suspended because of overdue payments.

You can also pay the auction site on an as-needed basis, on an auction-by-auction basis. You can pay with a cashier's check, money order, personal check, or credit card.

By the way, whether you check your account status or not, you'll still know how much you owe. Auction sites will bill you, often on a monthly basis, and let you know what's due.

Going, Going, Gone!

After the auction closes and there's been a high bidder, you'll have to get in touch with him and make arrangements for payment and shipping. The following is what to know and do:

• When the auction closes, you'll find out who the high bidder is and what the high bid is by checking your auction listing or by getting an email from the auction site.

• As soon as the auction closes, you should contact the high bidder with information including shipping fees, your address, how you want to be paid, and similar information.

- It's a good idea to check the high bidder's feedback so you can know how trustworthy he's likely to be.

- When you receive payment from the high bidder, you should notify him via email that you've received the payment. As soon as the payment clears, you should ship the item.

- After you've received payment and shipped the item, provide feedback about the buyer so that others can know if he's trustworthy.

- Remember to pay the auction site after your auction is complete; otherwise your privileges to bid and buy may be suspended.

CHAPTER 18

How to Accept Payment

You've done everything right with your auction—you've listed it, you've used techniques for creating a listing that drew bidders like bees to honey, and you've made contact with the seller. Now it's time to reap the fruits of your labor. It's time to accept payment.

In this chapter, you'll learn all you need to know about how to accept payment for your completed auction. You'll learn about all the different methods of payment, how you should handle each, and what you should do if you run into problems with the buyer.

Learn Basic Payment Etiquette

Before you learn how to accept payment, you'll need to know basic payment etiquette—what you should do when dealing with the buyer about money. Money is a touchy issue with many people, and you want to be sure that you get payment for your item, but you also want to make sure that the buyer is satisfied with the process of paying you or you'll get bad feedback on eBay. Include all the following steps, and you'll make sure you get paid and that the buyer will be happy with the transaction:

- *Make sure that you get paid in advance, including shipping charges*—As you learned earlier in the book, you should have made clear on your auction that the buyer will pay for shipping. When you sent your email to the buyer, you should also have told him that you require payment before you'll ship the item purchased. Wait until you get paid before shipping the goods—and you should get full payment, including shipping charges.

- *Ask that a description of the item accompany payment—* When someone pays you, you'll want a description of the

What You'll Learn in This Chapter

- The etiquette and rules you should follow when accepting payment from buyers.

- How you should handle accepting money orders and cashier's checks.

- Everything you need to know about accepting personal checks.

- How to handle Cash on Delivery (C.O.D.) payment.

- When to use escrow payment services, and why they can be good for sellers as well as buyers.

- What to do if you're having problems getting payment from the buyer.

- How you can get a refund if the high bidder refuses to send you payment.

item along with it, including the auction number. Otherwise, it will be difficult for you to keep track of what the payment is for, especially if you sell items on several different auctions. Make sure that the buyer also sends along his mailing address.

- *When the buyer contacts you to tell you payment is on the way, respond quickly*—Buyers are justifiably worried about who they're buying items from and will judge you according to how responsive you are to them. As soon as you get an email telling you the check is on the way, send back a note thanking the buyer for the message, and telling him that you'll be prompt in sending out the item to him after the payment arrives (or, in the case of a personal check, as soon as the check has cleared the bank).

- *When the payment arrives, send a note to the buyer*—As we all know, things get lost in the mail, and the buyer will want to make sure that his payment arrived in good order. When you receive payment, promptly send a note to the buyer stating that. Also tell him when you'll be shipping him the item, so that he'll know when to expect it.

You can accept credit cards at Amazon auctions

Amazon offers an extremely easy and inexpensive way for sellers to accept credit cards. Sellers pay 60 cents plus 4.75 percent of the transaction amount to accept a credit card, with no other fees charged.

You can accept credit cards for payment—for a fee

People prefer paying via credit cards to other forms of payment. But as an individual, you can't accept credit cards...or can you? Should you decide to go into selling via auctions full-time, you can set up a merchant account, which will allow you to accept credit card payments. You can set up these accounts straight from the Web. Some sites that allow you to do this include *www.ezmerchantaccounts.com, www.merchantaccount.com, www.interlinkmerchant.com,*and *www.1stamericancardservice.com.*

Keep in mind, though, that setting up a merchant account is not cheap and can eat into your profits. Some sites charge hundreds of dollars for a setup fee in addition to normal ongoing fees. Even if no setup fee is charged, you'll still get hit with good-sized charges. For example, one of the lowest-cost merchant accounts I've found, *www.1stamericancardservice.com*, doesn't charge a setup fee, but takes 2.44 percent of all your sales, charges a 30 cent fee for each transaction, and charged a $9 monthly "statement fee." You'll have to pay them a minimum fee of $20 a month, whether you rack up $20 in charges or not.

Money Orders and Cashier's Checks: The Gold Standard for Accepting Payment

The easiest ways to accept payment are money orders and cashier's checks. For sellers, they're the gold standard, because they're as good as cash and don't have any of the drawbacks of sending cash through the mail.

When you get a money order, it has an identification number. The buyer has a receipt that includes the identification number as well, so the check can be traced, if there's a problem with it, or so the seller can get a replacement for the money order if it's lost in the mail.

A money order is, in essence, cash. The seller has paid cash for it, and you can cash it at your bank or other financial institution. You won't have to wait for it to clear, as you do with a personal check. Instead, the money is yours immediately. Because of this, you want to encourage buyers to pay via money order. A good incentive is to promise to ship the goods within 24 hours of receiving the money order.

Cashier's checks are similar—they can only be issued when the seller has enough money in the bank to cover the check. As a result, they're in essence as good as cash as well—or almost. To make sure that they're not counterfeit, wait until you've deposited them before shipping anything out.

What You Need to Know About Accepting Personal Checks

Most people on auction sites prefer paying by personal check. They're the least trouble for most people—not having to go to a bank or post office to get a money order or cashier's check.

Because of that, you might have to accept personal checks instead of money orders or cashier's checks at your auction. If you say on your auction listing that you won't accept personal checks, you're conceivably cutting down on your potential audience, so you might have to accept personal checks.

In general, the only issue you'll have accepting personal checks is that they can bounce. Because checks can bounce, never ship an item until a check clears. When you talk to the buyer about

You can accept money from international buyers

If the buyer is in a different country than you, he can pay with an international money order. The buyer gets a money order in his own currency. You take it to your bank and can convert it into cash.

payment, make it clear that you won't be shipping out an item until the check clears.

Ask your bank whether the money is in your account

Because of legal requirements, a bank may report to you that a check has cleared even though the money is not yet in your account. Before shipping an item, make sure the money is actually in your account.

For what to do about bounced checks, turn to the section titled "How To Deal with Payment Problems" later in this chapter.

How to Deal with C.O.D. Payment

Another popular payment method some buyers prefer is Cash on Delivery, commonly called C.O.D. If you have a buyer who insists on C.O.D., you should insist that they pay the extra C.O.D. charge. When a buyer pays via C.O.D., you ship the item as C.O.D., and then the buyer gets the item and pays the shipper the price of your item plus the extra C.O.D. charges. Again, if a buyer insists on this form of payment, the buyer should pay the extra charges.

Using Escrow Services

If you're selling a big-ticket item, the buyer may want to use an escrow service. An escrow service serves as a go-between between you and the buyer. It assures the buyer that he won't get burned because you only get payment once the goods are received and accepted by the buyer. The buyer pays the escrow service, and the escrow service in turn pays you once the item has been received and inspected by the buyer.

It's clear why an escrow service is good for a buyer. But escrow services are also good for sellers when you're selling a big-ticket item. They offer the following benefits for sellers:

- *It allows buyers to pay via credit card*—Unless you've set up a special merchant account with a credit card company, buyers won't be able to pay you with a credit card. With escrow services, though, the buyer pays the escrow service using a credit card, and the service in turn pays you, so the buyer will be able to pay for the item via a credit card. This is important when big-ticket items are being sold.

- *It makes sure that you won't have to deal with bad checks or other payment headaches*—Bad checks are a particular problem. Not only will you not get the money for the item you want to sell, but banks may charge you a fee for depositing a bad check. Because the escrow service only tells you to send the goods after it receives payment, you won't ever have to deal with bad checks.

- *It insures your goods when you ship*—You won't have to arrange for shipping insurance. The escrow service does that for you.

Escrow services charge fees depending on the selling cost of an item. A typical fee is five percent of the cost of the item, with a $5 minimum fee. Several well-known escrow services are *www.iescrow.com*, *www.trade-direct.com*, and *www.tradesafe.com*. The next figure shows the *www.iescrow.com* Web site.

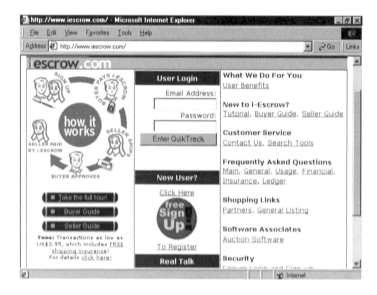

For safety in big-ticket transactions, many buyers and sellers prefer to use an escrow site such as www. iescrow.com.

If a buyer wants to use an escrow service, make sure that it's clear who's paying the extra amount for the escrow service. In general, buyers pay for extra services on auction sites, so try to get the buyer to pay the whole amount. However, if you want to get a buyer to use the service, you may have to pay for part or all of the fee.

There's a lot more to learn about escrow services. For more information, turn to Chapter 21, "Protecting Yourself Through Escrow Services."

Escrow services often have strict shipping guidelines

You'll need to pay special attention to how you ship items when you're dealing with an escrow service. They often have strict shipping guidelines, including how you have to package the goods and which shipping companies you're allowed to use. So when packing up your item and arranging for shipping, make sure you are following the escrow service rules.

How to Deal with Payment Problems

In the vast majority of cases, you won't run into trouble when accepting payment for an item. But there's a chance that you will. You may have to deal with bounced checks or high bidders who simply won't pay up or respond to your email after they've won. In this section, I'll teach you how to handle these kinds of problems. For more information about how to avoid getting burned as a seller and what to do if you are burned, turn to Chapter 20, "How to Avoid Getting Burned."

How to Handle Bad Checks

There's a chance that when someone sends you a personal check for payment, it will be a bad one and will bounce. That's bad on two counts. First, you haven't gotten your money for the auction. Secondly, your bank often will charge you a fee for depositing the bad check.

If you receive a bad check, don't assume the worst—that the buyer was trying to scam you. Instead, send a polite note to the buyer, telling him that his check didn't clear the bank, and informing him that you'd like him to send another check and to reimburse you for the bad-check fee your bank charged you. In most instances, this should clear up the problem—the buyer will be more embarrassed than anything else and will send along payment.

Make clear to the buyer that you don't want cash

Cash is bad because it can be stolen or lost when it's sent via the mail, and there's no "paper trail" to follow should a dispute arise between buyer and seller. Make it clear to the buyer that you don't accept cash.

You may get a buyer who tries to convince you to send the item anyway, saying that he'll send the check immediately. If you could find someone who tries to sweet-talk you in some other way to convince you to send the item out, don't do it. Only send out the item after you've received a good check and received reimbursement for the bad one.

If, after some back-and-forth, the buyer doesn't send a good check and reimburse you for the bad one, it's time to cut your losses. Send a polite but firm note saying you want full payment and reimbursement, and that if you don't get it, you'll cancel his high bid and leave negative feedback about him on eBay. Give him a specific time period in which to send the money. If you don't get it, leave negative feedback. You can then either inform

the second-high bidder that the item is available to him or her for
sale, or you can ask your auction site to reimburse you for the
cost you paid for listing the item instead. Some auction sites,
including eBay, let you get reimbursement for a variety of reasons, including receiving a bad check. I'll show you how to do it
later in this chapter.

What to Do If the Buyer Never Responds to You

In some instances, it's possible that the buyer will not respond to
your emails and there's no way for you to get payment. If the
buyer doesn't respond to your first note, follow up with a second
one several days later. Then try a third a week after that. By the
way, keep in mind that some buyers may be more casual about
checking and replying to their email than sellers are. Some people
(like me) check their email frequently throughout the day, while
other people may check their email only once every few days. If
you don't hear back from a buyer within a few days of your sending an email message, it may only mean that he hasn't checked
his email recently.

On that note, warn the buyer that if you don't hear back within a
certain amount of time, you're canceling his bid and leaving negative feedback about him or her on eBay. If you don't hear back,
do what you do when dealing with someone who won't make
good on a bad check: Inform the second-high bidder that the item
is available for sale, or get the auction site to reimburse you for
the fee you paid for listing the item.

How to Get Reimbursed If There Are Payment Problems

If you have payment problems, don't despair: Many auction sites,
like eBay, will reimburse you if things go bad for payment problems or other reasons. Each site has different guidelines on when
you can ask for reimbursement. The following are eBay's guidelines, taken word-for-word from its Web site, on when you can
ask for a full refund. If you're using another site, check to see its
guidelines.

- High bidder did not respond after you attempted to contact
  them. (Please allow at least 7 days for them to respond).

- High bidder "backed out" and did not buy item.

- High bidder's check bounced or they placed a stop payment on it.

- High bidder returned item and you issued a refund.

- High bidder could not complete auction due to family or financial emergency.

- High bidder claimed terms were unacceptable.

You'll get a refund on what eBay calls the Final Value Fee Credit. This is the fee you pay eBay that's calculated as a percentage of your final selling price. You won't get refunds for the insertion fee, which is the small, nominal fee that you pay to initiate the auction. You also won't get refunds for other fees such as the fee you pay to add boldface to your auction, to get the item featured, or similar fees.

To get your refund on eBay, you'll have to fill out the form that you see in the following figure.

Here's hoping you never have to use a form like this: You'll fill this out when requesting a refund for an auction gone bad on eBay.

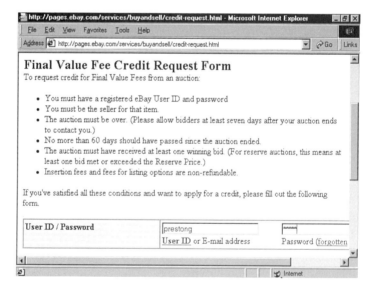

To get to the form, click Services from the main page of eBay, click Buying and Selling, and then click Request Final Value Fee Credit. You'll find information on that page about how to get your credit. There are a variety of simple rules you'll have to follow to get the reimbursement; they'll all be listed there. You can also get partial reimbursement in some situations. The page will explain why and how.

Going, Going, Gone!

After the auction closes and you make contact with the bidder, you'll make arrangements for payment, accept the money, and then ship out the item. The following summarizes what you need to know:

- Don't ship out an item until you get paid—and if you're being paid by personal check, don't send it until the check clears.

- Respond quickly to buyers when they send you email, and alert them when you've received payment and when you're shipping their item. In this way, you'll receive good feedback on your auction site, and future bidders will learn to trust you.

- Money orders and cashier's checks are great methods of payment because they're, in essence, as good as cash. To encourage buyers to pay in this manner, guarantee shipment of the item the same day you receive the money order or cashier's check.

- Escrow services are a good choice for payment for big-ticket items. They serve as a go-between between you and the buyer, and resolve any issues that may arise. They will also accept credit cards, so it's a good way for a buyer to pay for a big-ticket item with his credit card.

- If the buyer send a personal check that doesn't clear, ask that he send a new check and reimburse you for the fee your bank charges you for handling the bad check.

- If for some reason the buyer doesn't send payment or refuses to answer your emails, you can usually get a refund on the fee you pay your auction site.

CHAPTER 19

How to Ship Your Items

New sellers at auctions think a lot about how to create auctions that sell, and may concern themselves with how to accept payment. But odds are that they spend little time, if any at all, preparing for shipping the items they've sold.

Don't let yourself fall into that trap. For sellers, shipping can be the most important part of the deal in many ways. If the goods are damaged or lost en route to the buyer, or if they're late getting there, you'll end up with an unhappy buyer, may be in a situation where you'll be forced to reimburse him, and you could end up with bad ratings on an auction site. If this happens, you'll have a very short life, indeed, as a successful auctioneer.

In this chapter, you'll learn all you need to know about shipping items, from what supplies you'll need, how to package the goods, how to find a shipper, and more.

Four Rules to Follow When Shipping

Before we get down to the nitty-gritty of actual shipping, there's a few general rules you should know about shipping. If you follow these four rules, you'll be well on your way to successfully shipping your items and keeping your buyers satisfied:

- *Rule Number One: Be prepared*—This motto should hold for auctioneers, not just Boy Scouts. Well before your auction closes, have your packing materials on hand. Know how fragile the item is that you're shipping and be ready to package it properly. Before the auction ends, know how you'll ship it.

- *Rule Number Two: Pack it carefully*—What happens if the item is damaged during shipment? You end up with a very unhappy buyer who may demand a refund. So take extra care when packing an item. Err on the side of being too careful. It's worth the extra time.

- *Rule Number Three: Send it out as soon as payment clears—* Buyers understandably want to get their hands on what they've bought as quickly as possible. The longer they wait, the more nervous they get that the item won't arrive—and the less likely they are to give you positive feedback. So as soon as the payment clears, send out the item. For you, shipping may be an afterthought; for the buyer, it's the whole point of the auction.

- *Rule Number Four: Considering registering or insuring the package—*There are ways, including sending the item as registered or insuring it, to make sure that you'll know the item gets to the buyer in good shape or to cover yourself if it doesn't. It costs extra to do this, and you may consider asking the buyer to take on the extra costs. If it's an expensive item, you may eat the costs yourself. Later in this chapter, I'll go into more detail about your options when sending items registered or insured.

Where to Get Shipping Supplies

One of the hidden costs of selling items is the cost of shipping supplies. All those boxes, packing tape, and other things you'll need can add up pretty quickly. In this section I'll teach you where to get shipping supplies—in particular, how to get them for free.

Scavenging Supplies for Free

Before going out and buying supplies, see what you have around the house that can be recycled. Almost anything that you buy new will be packed in a box, so save those boxes. If space is a problem where you live, and you can't store them all, take off the tape holding the box together, if any, and fold the boxes flat. You can store many boxes when they're flat.

Take cast-off boxes and supplies home from work to cut down on shipping supply costs

One of the best places to get no-cost supplies is your place of work. No, I'm not suggesting that you take new supplies home and use them—but at most offices, an enormous amount of material, such as boxes, is thrown away. Office supplies, computers, software, printers, and other office equipment come in boxes that are usually discarded. Much of this material makes great shipping supplies.

Check for boxes that are being thrown away. A real find are boxes that have Styrofoam packing "peanuts" in them. These are great for protecting items that you ship. Also look for bubble wrap, oversized heavy-duty envelopes, and anything else that looks like it will do the trick.

Before taking anything home from the office, of course, check to make sure you're allowed to do it. In fact, if you check with your office manager and tell him or her what you plan to do, you can make an arrangement to take as much of the discards home as you can on a regular basis.

If you buy goods via mail-order or over the Web—or if you buy at auctions—you have a ready-made supply of supplies. Don't throw away the boxes, bubble wrap, "peanuts," and similar items that you receive when things are delivered to you via the mail.

Ask friends to save the supplies for you as well. Yes, you may have to swallow your pride a little when asking, but they'll be happy to comply. After all, what are friends for?

Retail stores in your town or neighborhood are good sources of supplies as well. In particular, they'll have many boxes that they throw away on a regular basis.

When recycling shipping supplies like this, be sure that the boxes or supplies are in good shape. Carefully examine the boxes to make sure that they're not torn or worn, and that they're still sturdy enough to protect the goods you're shipping.

Getting Free Supplies from Shippers

Before you go out and buy supplies, check with your shipper to see what they supply. Many shippers supply a wide range of free items. The U.S. Postal Service, for example, provides some kinds of free supplies when you ship via Priority Mail and Express Mail. Services like Airborne Express and Federal Express also offer free packaging. Check at your local post office or call your shipping company.

Paying for the Supplies

Get free supplies from the Web

You can order supplies from the U.S. Postal Service on the Web at *www.usps.gov*. They'll be sent to you for free.

You won't always be able to get free supplies from your office, home, or from shippers. In that case, you'll have to pay for them. Your local office supply store will be well-stocked and is also a good place to turn. Also, look for stores such as Mailboxes Etc. that specialize in shipping goods—they always have a big selection of shipping supplies. You can reach the company on the Internet at *www.mbe.com*. You also can order shipping supplies online at office supply sites such as *www.staples.com* and *www.officedepot.com*.

What Supplies You'll Need

While the kind of supplies you'll need to keep on hand will vary according to what you're shipping, here's a good starting point. Keep these items on hand and you'll be well-prepared for most kinds of shipping:

- Various sized boxes
- Clear shipping tape
- Utility knife
- Nine-inch by twelve-inch manila envelopes
- Black permanent markers
- Self-adhesive shipping labels
- Business cards, if you have any
- Bubble wrap
- Filling material, such as Styrofoam "peanuts"

Armed with all that, you're ready to ship. In the next section, you'll learn the basics of shipping various kinds of items.

How to Pack the Goods to Be Shipped

With several million items for sale every day on eBay, the array of goods that auctioneers ship is truly mind-boggling. There's really no way to do justice to all the kinds of things that can be shipped. But keep the following tips in mind when packing the goods, and you'll go a long way toward making sure that they'll be received safely and securely:

- *Always assume that packages will be dropped, thrown, and manhandled*—In everything you do, use more packaging material rather than less to keep the item safe.

- *Ship fragile items in a box inside a box*—If you're shipping glass, pottery, or similarly fragile items, use the two-box method. First wrap the fragile item in bubble wrap or a similar material. Then put it in a box filled with "peanuts" or a similar protective material and seal up the box. Put that box, in turn, inside a larger box filled with "peanuts" or protective material. Finally, seal the larger box.

- *Put goods like Beanie Babies inside a sealed, protective plastic bag, and buy a tag protector to protect the tag*—(Beanie collectors prize tags that are as new-looking as possible.) Then protect it with "peanuts" or similar filling material inside a box and seal.

- *Put collectible cards such as baseball cards and Pokémon cards inside special hard, protective sleeves before shipping them*—These sleeves will make sure that the cards aren't damaged when they're shipped. Make sure, however, to pack protective material around them, or to ship them in an shipping envelope that contains protective material to make sure no damage occurs.

- *Protect flat items like photographs and small posters by placing them between two pieces of sturdy cardboard*—You don't want the items to be bent when they're shipped.

- *You can ship posters in cardboard tubes*—Cardboard tubes do a good job of protecting posters. The posters will be curled when they arrive, but they'll soon flatten out.

Include a personal note and business card with the item

Selling isn't just about making a single sale, it's about developing relationships. So include a note with the item you ship, thanking the buyer for payment and including your contact information and a business card.

Deciding Which Shipper to Use

There are many different shippers to choose from, including the U.S. Postal Service (*www.usps.gov*), Federal Express (*www.fedex.com*), Airborne Express (*www.airborne.com*), and

United Parcel Service (*www.ups.com*), among others. While there
are differences among them, those differences aren't dramatic
enough to make one much better than another—here's an instance
where your personal preference should take precedence. Take into
account how convenient the shipper is to you, whether they'll
pick up from your house, and similar things. Depending on where
and what you're shipping, the rates of all the carriers will vary.

**UPS and Federal
Express don't ship to
P.O. boxes**

If the buyer has a
P.O. box, you'll have
to ship it using the
U.S. Postal Service.
Most shipping com-
panies, including
United Parcel Service
and Federal Express,
don't ship to them.

Whichever you choose, though, make sure that the shipper lets
you track the status of your package, and that it has a return
receipt capability, so that if you want, you can make sure you'll
know when the goods are delivered. Also, be aware that what
method you choose to ship should take into account the buyer's
preferences as well. If the buyer lives in an area that a particular
delivery service doesn't go to, or that causes difficulty in some
other way for the buyer, you'll need to use a different method of
shipment. Also keep in mind that if on your auction page you let
potential bidders know that you're flexible in how you'll ship
items, you're more likely to attract more bidders and should get
higher prices on your items.

One of the best ways to handle shipping is to use one of the new
Internet shipping services. These excellent sites will compare
costs of different shipping services for you, based on the package
weight, where you're shipping from, and where you're shipping
to. Then, straight from the site, you can schedule a pickup and
track your packages as well. Good ones include the following:

- *www.auctionship.com*

- *www.intershipper.net*

- *www.smartship.com*

- *www.iship.com*

The following figure shows the *www.iship.com* Web site—it
shows delivery times and rates for sending a six-pound package.

How to determine shipping costs ahead of time

For sellers, it's a bit of a Catch-22: You tell buyers on your auction page
that you want them to pay for shipping before you'll ship the item, but
how can you know how much shipping will cost until you take the

package to the shipper? You could take the package to the shipper before you post your auction to get a cost estimate, but that means an extra trip because you'll have to take it back again when you actually ship the item.

A simpler way: Buy a low-cost shipping scale from an office supply store. Then weigh the item along with the packaging that you'll ship it in. After you know the weight of the item, you can easily get the price from a shipper. Additionally, you can always visit one of the online shipping sites that will tell you charges of various shippers based on the weight of the package you're shipping.

Using an Internet shipping service like www.iship.com can help you find the best shipper at the best price— and you can arrange for pickup and track your packages from the site as well.

Should You Register and Insure Packages?

As I said earlier in the chapter, expect that whatever package you ship will get kicked around en route to its final destination. That means that it could be damaged, so you should consider insuring your package. Insurance is generally inexpensive, and, depending on the cost of your item, can be as low as 75 cents, or free, if you ship via UPS and your item has a value less than $100.

Who should pay for insurance? You can make it clear on your auction listing that the buyer can pay for insurance if he wants the item insured. But the truth is, it's your responsibility to get the item safely to the buyer, so you might want to pay for insurance regardless of whether the buyer decides to pay for it.

If you're shipping a high-cost item and want to be absolutely sure that you know when it gets to the buyer, you can register it and send it via the Post Office as Return Receipt Requested. That way, you'll know that when the item was received. Keep in mind that when you're shipping via the Postal Service, the package will take longer to get to its final destination when you register and/or insure the item.

Going, Going, Gone!

After you've received payment and deposited it, it's time to ship the goods. Keep in mind the following when shipping your items:

- Always have shipping supplies on-hand, including boxes, clear tape, and Styrofoam "peanuts," and so on.

- You can get much of your shipping supplies for free by saving boxes from around your house and by checking at work to see what kind of boxes and supplies they're discarding. Local office supply stores offer shipping supplies for sale, as do Web sites such as *www.staples.com* and *www.officedepot.com*.

- When you ship items, assume that they'll be dropped and otherwise manhandled. So make sure to pack the items securely using plenty of packing material, bubble wrap, and so on.

- Compare prices and services of shippers before shipping, but use the one that is most convenient for you and will let you track your packages. You can compare prices of the different shippers and even arrange shipping online via several Web sites including *www.auctionship.com*, *www.iship.com*, *www.intershipper.net*, and *www.smartship.com*.

- It's a good idea to insure high-cost items because it's your responsibility to make sure it gets to the buyer safely. If you decide to insure an item, be sure to ask the buyer if he's interested in paying for the insurance.

PART 5

Caveat Emptor

CHAPTER 20

How to Avoid Getting Burned

When you buy or sell at an auction site, you're generally safe. In the vast majority of auctions, the sale goes off without a hitch.

But while most auctions are safe, sometimes you may get burned. While only an extremely small percentage of auctions cause problems, so many millions of auctions take place every day online that auction fraud is perhaps the most common consumer complaint on the Internet.

In this chapter, you'll learn how to make sure that you never get burned at an Internet auction. Additionally, in the unlikely event that you do get burned, you'll learn how to fight back.

The Ways You Can Get Burned at an Auction Site

While auction sites are generally safe, there are still a number of ways you can get burned if you're buying and selling at them. In this section, you'll learn the ways that both buyers and sellers can get burned at auction sites.

What Buyers Need to Watch Out For on Auction Sites

The most common auction scams reported happen to buyers, not sellers. The following are some things that can happen to buyers at auction sites:

- *The seller never delivers the goods*—The buyer sends money, and the seller never ships the item.

- *The goods that are shipped aren't what was promised by the seller at the auction*—For example, the goods may be damaged, were either promised as new but in fact were used, or were simply lied about. In one of the most notorious instances of this, a buyer on eBay paid $1,815 as a high bidder for what she was told was a rare "Quackers" duck Beanie Baby made without wings. What was delivered to her, instead, was a $5 version with the wings hacked off.

Auction scams are the most commonly reported frauds on the Internet

Internet Fraud Watch (*www.fraud.org*) reports that the most commonly reported Internet scams are auction frauds: people who don't receive items that they've paid for and people who receive items that weren't what was promised.

- *The goods were described in a misleading way in the auction listing*—While the description may have been technically accurate, in subtle and not-so-subtle ways, it was implied that the goods were really more valuable than they were worth. This can be a particular problem when buying collectibles.

- *You are charged and then wait forever for your item*—If you're buying from the auction site, rather than a person, the site immediately charged your credit card, and then didn't ship the goods for a long time.

- *The seller sells illegal goods*—Pirated software and movies are often sold on auction sites, and are just some of the illegal goods being sold online. You often won't know ahead of time that what you're buying is illegal.

What Sellers Need to Watch Out For at Auction Sites

There are fewer scams involving sellers at auctions, but there are still some things that sellers need to watch out for as well:

- *You can be the victim of "shielding" or "shield bidding"*—In this scam, two people work together. The first person places a low, winning bid early in the bidding process. Next the second person makes an extremely high bid on the item, scaring away other potential bidders. Then, at the last moment, the second bidder pulls out, and the seller is forced to sell the item to the first, lower bidder.

- *The buyer may never pay you, or may send you a check that doesn't clear*—When this happens, the seller can try to sell the item to the next-high bidder, but won't always be able to do that.

What You Can Do to Avoid Getting Burned

The odds are great that you won't be involved with a problem when bidding or buying at an auction site. But if you want to do everything possible to make sure you don't get burned at an auction site, the following are some thing you should do:

- *Investigate the buyer or the seller*—Check the feedback on the auction site to see if they have received negative comments (see the next figure for an example of such a page on eBay). If there are many comments, you'll know to be wary of dealing with them. At some sites, such as eBay, someone can change their user ID to a new one, which means that all their old feedback will vanish. When that happens on eBay, a small picture of sunglasses will appear next to their name. Be careful when dealing with people who have changed identities in this way.

- *Get identifying information about the seller*—If you're suspicious, ask for a name, address, and phone number, and then call the seller's phone number or check with directory assistance to make sure the phone number is a valid one.

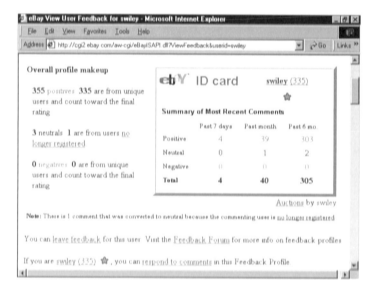

Here's how you'll investigate someone's feedback on eBay. Checking out a buyer or seller is one of the best ways to make sure you don't get burned at an auction site.

- *Be wary of people who ask to be paid in cash*—There's no reason to pay in cash, and no way to track that your payment has been made. Don't pay cash. And don't bid in auctions where the seller doesn't clearly indicate that he accepts payment methods other than cash.

- *Use escrow services for buying big-ticket items and when you're uneasy about the seller*—If you're a buyer, escrow services hold your money until you've received the goods and say they're what you've been promised. Chapter 21, "Protecting Yourself Through Escrow Services," teaches you how to use them.

- *When you can, pay with a credit card*—Credit cards offer consumer protection that other forms of payment don't. If you're buying directly from an auction site instead of a person, or you're buying from a business on a person-to-person auction site such as eBay, pay with a credit card.

- *Ask to pay via C.O.D.*—With C.O.D., you only pay for an item when you receive it. It's a good way for sellers to guarantee that they receive something. It's not a perfect guarantee, however, because the buyer typically cannot open the package and inspect its contents before paying for it. C.O.D. protects the buyer against getting nothing at all, but not against getting an item that's damaged or not what was ordered.

- *Check the auction site's insurance policy*—Sites such as eBay and Amazon include insurance policies that cover part or all of what you'll pay for an item if it's never delivered to you. Before bidding and buying, check the auction site's insurance policy to make sure that it'll cover you if you're burned. Chapter 22, "Using Appraisal Firms, Verification Services, and Insurance," gives more details about auction insurance.

- *If you're buying from the auction site or from a business on a person-to-person site, ask for the return policy and warranty*—When you buy from the site or a business, you should expect to get a warranty and often you'll be able to return items. Get it in writing before bidding.

- *Be especially careful when buying collectibles*—You're not going to be able to examine the item before bidding, so be

Take note when a buyer or bidder has a free email account

It's easy for anyone to get a free email account at the many dozens of sites that give them out, such as *www.hotmail.com*, *www.yahoo.com*, *www.bigfoot.com*, and many others. When someone gets a free email account at one of these sites, there's no way to verify their identity—track them down. Additionally, there's no verifying information such as a credit card number. Because of that, it's easy for someone to use a free email account, pull a scam, and then never use the account again. Just because someone has a free account doesn't mean that they're not on the up-and-up, but if you see negative feedback combined with an email address at a free email account, that should raise a big red flag.

especially careful when buying a collectible at an auction. Ask that a trusted appraisal service verify the item, and get a written statement about the appraisal before bidding. Pay using an escrow service because that way you'll have several days to examine the item—and get it appraised yourself—before deciding whether it's the genuine article. Chapter 22 gives more details about these firms.

• *Don't bid on or sell banned items*—Many auction sites ban certain items from being sold on them, such as firearms, alcohol, tobacco, and other items. Find the list of banned items, and make sure to never put them up for sale or buy them. If you do, you may be banned from the auction site—and you won't get any kind of insurance protection should you buy or sell a banned item.

• *Beware if there's a big discrepancy between the retail price of a piece of software being sold and the asking price on an auction site*—If the software retails for $599 and the asking price is $15, you can be sure there's a problem—more likely than not, the software is illegally pirated.

• *Keep printed records about every transaction*—Save all email between you and the buyer or seller and print it out. Also print out the auction listing and the end of auction listing on the site itself. You'll need it if you need to make a complaint against the buyer or seller.

How to Spot an Illegal Item for Sale

As a potential buyer, you don't want to bid on illegal items or items that have been banned by auction sites. Among other problems this would cause, you will lose any insurance the site offers. And someone offering an illegal or banned item for sale will be more likely than the average auctioneer to perpetrate an auction scam.

Each auction site has different items they ban. It's always a good idea to check the auction site to see what it allows to be sold.

eBay is typical of many auction sites. The following are some of the items that aren't allowed to be sold on eBay. For a more comprehensive listing, check the site.

- Animals and animal parts

- Firearms

- Fireworks

- Government IDs and licenses

- Human parts and remains

- Current stock and stock certificates

- Surveillance equipment

- TV descramblers

- Alcohol

- Tobacco

- Software or music on CD-R (CD-ROMs that can be copied on a computer)

- 35mm and 70mm movie prints

More than half the software sold at auctions is illegal

The Software & Information Industry Association (SIAA) found that at least 60 percent of the software being sold on auction sites is pirated and is therefore illegal. Before bidding, ask the buyer if the item is shrink-wrapped and, therefore, legal.

Note that eBay allows software to be sold, as long as it's not on CD-R, but you should still be careful when buying software because it may be illegally pirated.

What You Can Do If You've Been Burned

It may be that despite your best efforts, you've been burned—for example, the seller has taken the money and run. There are still things you can do to try and recoup your money, or at a minimum try to get the offender prosecuted. The following are the steps you can take if you've been burned or suspect that you've been burned on an auction site.

Before making complaints as outlined next, gather all the correspondence between you and the seller and print it all out. Check with your bank or financial institution to see if your personal check, cashier's check, or money order has been cashed, and get any information about it. Contact the seller and warn him you're going to have him investigated unless he resolves the matter to your satisfaction. If that fails here's what you can do:

- Report the suspected fraud to the auction site. Many auction sites will investigate complaints of fraud. On eBay, for example, send a complaint to *safeharbor@ebay.com*, and include all relevant information, including your auction number and all email communication involved in the auction.

- If you mailed payment via the U.S. Postal Service, and the seller claims that he never received payment but your cashier's check or money order has been cashed, you can file a Lost Mail Claim at the post office. As part of the postal investigation, the seller will have to fill out a form saying that the payment was never received. While the investigation may never turn something up, it may force the seller to think twice about perjuring himself during an investigation and may suddenly "find" the payment he thought he never received.

- If you suspect fraud and you mailed your payment via the U.S. mail, you can fill out a mail fraud form and ask that it be investigated. Go to your local post office to get a copy of the form.

- Report the fraud to the National Fraud Information Center at *www.fraud.org* or by calling (800) 876-7060. The following figure shows the Web site.

Here's how you'll report suspected fraud on an auction site to the National Fraud Information Center.

- Report the fraud to the Federal Trade Commission, a federal agency charged with investigating some forms of Internet fraud. You can reach the agency at *www.ftc.gov* and file a complaint online.

- Report the fraud to your state attorney general or county district attorney. Then send a copy of your complaint to eBay at:

  ATTN: Fraud Prevention

  eBay

  2005 Hamilton Avenue, Suite 350

  San Jose, CA 95125

Going, Going, Gone!

You want to make sure that you never get ripped off at an auction site. To make sure you never get burned, follow this advice.

- Check out a seller's or buyer's feedback on an auction site. If there's negative feedback, don't bid, and be very leery about dealing with them if you're the seller.

- Never pay with cash. It's impossible to trace, and if you pay with cash, you can easily become the victim of a scam.

- Use escrow services to pay for big-ticket items when you're leery about paying the seller directly or when you're buying collectibles.

- When possible, pay with a credit card when buying directly from the auction site or from a business on a person-to-person auction site.

- Make sure that you know a site's insurance policy before bidding. Also know what items aren't allowed to be sold on the site—if you pay for one of them, you won't be insured.

- If you've been the victim of a scam, report it to the auction site, to law enforcement agencies, and to other agencies that investigate Internet fraud. Be sure to print out and provide copies of all correspondence related to the fraud and any other relevant materials.

CHAPTER 21

Protecting Yourself Through Escrow Services

If you're buying a big-ticket item, or for some reason are concerned that the seller of the goods you've just won at an auction won't come through with the goods after you send payment, you should use an escrow service. Escrow services protect buyers from unscrupulous sellers. Additionally, as you'll see in this chapter, they can help sellers as well.

In this chapter, you'll learn what escrow services are, how to use them, and you'll see the differences among the top escrow services.

What Are Escrow Services?

Escrow services are businesses that serve as intermediaries between buyers and sellers. They make sure that both buyers and sellers are protected from being taken for a ride or are unhappy with the transaction.

In an escrow transaction, the buyer pays the escrow service, which, in turn, holds the payment from the seller until the goods are shipped. Then, once the buyer receives the goods and is happy with them, the escrow service pays the seller. The escrow service charges a fee for its services.

These kinds of services are particularly useful for big-ticket items. If there's a lot of money involved in a transaction, the buyer, in particular, will want to know that the seller won't take the money and never ship the goods.

But there are benefits for both buyers and sellers when using escrow services. The following sections discuss the reasons buyers and sellers will benefit from using escrow services.

What You'll Learn in This Chapter

▶ What escrow services are, and why they're good for both buyers and sellers.

▶ How escrow services work.

▶ When you should—and shouldn't—use an escrow service.

▶ How you'll use an escrow service.

▶ How to compare the top escrow services.

Why Escrow Services Are Good for Buyers

Buyers of big-ticket items, in particular, should consider using an escrow service. The following are all the reasons why escrow services are good for buyers:

- *Escrow services make sure that the buyer won't get taken for a ride by the seller*—Because the escrow service only releases the payment after the goods have been received and the seller has verified that they were what was expected, the buyer knows that he'll get what he paid for.

- *Escrow services allow the buyer to pay via credit card, even when the seller doesn't accept that form of payment*—Many people prefer paying by credit card to any other form of payment. Individuals normally don't accept credit cards, so it's rare at person-to-person auctions that buyers can use their credit cards. Because escrow services accept credit cards, it means that sellers can pay via credit card when they otherwise normally wouldn't have been able to do so.

Why Escrow Services Are Good for Sellers

At first, you might think that escrow services are good only for buyers. In fact, these services offer benefits to sellers as well. The following are the reasons why escrow services are often a good deal if you're the seller:

You don't have to use a credit card to pay an escrow service

Escrow services take several forms of payment, including money orders, cashier's check, and electronic wiring of funds. Some will take personal checks as well, although the transaction can't proceed until after the check clears.

- *Escrow services allow sellers to, in essence, accept payment via credit card*—If you're running a big-ticket auction, people may be wary of paying via any way other than credit card. Because the buyer pays the escrow service via credit card, that means that the seller can, in essence, accept payment that way.

- *Escrow services ensure that sellers don't have to worry about payment headaches*—Bad checks and other payment nightmares are the bane of a seller's existence. With an escrow service, the seller doesn't have to worry about payment problems. Because the payment is done via credit card, the seller is guaranteed payment.

- *The escrow service often arranges for shipping insurance—* This means that the seller won't have to go to the extra step of arranging for insurance.

How Escrow Services Work

Paying via escrow services is a simple process, and all work pretty much the same. The following is a step-by-step look at how an escrow service works:

1. The buyer and seller agree that payment will be made via an escrow service and agree who will bear the extra costs.

2. The buyer pays the escrow service the final bidding price of the item, plus the escrow fee (if that was what was agreed to in step 1).

3. The escrow service tells the seller that it's received payment.

4. The seller ships the goods to the buyer.

5. The buyer receives the goods and tells the escrow service that the goods arrived and were what was promised.

6. The escrow service pays the seller. If the buyer and seller agreed that the seller would bear some or all of the extra escrow costs, the seller pays that money to the buyer.

When You Should Use an Escrow Service

An escrow service helps make buying and selling at auctions more secure. But they do add costs to every transaction for which they're used. You shouldn't use escrow services for every transaction—and, in fact, you shouldn't use escrow services for most transactions. When should you use an escrow service, and when shouldn't you? The following is a list of things you need to know:

- *Don't use escrow services for low-cost items, especially if both bidder and seller have positive feedback—*Most escrow services charge a minimum charge of at least $5 and sometimes more. For lost-cost items, it doesn't make sense to use an escrow service, especially if bidder and seller both have positive track records.

The buyer usually pays the escrow fee

While the buyer and seller at an auction can make any kind of arrangements they want, the common rule is that the buyer pays the escrow fee.

- *If you and the seller (or you and the bidder) have dealt with each other in the past, you may not need to use an escrow service*—If you've done business with someone else on an auction site frequently, you probably won't need an escrow service when dealing with them again. However, if it's a big-ticket item, you're still taking a chance.

- *Buyers should use an escrow service for big-ticket items*—It's not important for sellers to use an escrow service for big-ticket items because they'll receive payment before they ship. But buyers should always use an escrow service for any big-ticket item.

- *Buyers should use an escrow service when buying collectibles*—When you buy collectibles at an online auction, you don't get to examine the goods ahead of time to verify that the collectible is the real thing. If you use an escrow service when buying collectibles, though, you get to examine the goods before allowing the service to release your payment.

Use escrow services with overseas buyers

An escrow service works well when an overseas buyer wants to pay you in his own currency. The buyer pays the escrow service, and the escrow service will pay you in U.S. funds.

- *If you're a buyer and you don't trust the seller, use an escrow service*—You don't have to use escrow services only for big ticket items. If you're a buyer, and there's something you want badly but the seller has mixed feedback, you'll want to use an escrow service

- *If you're a seller, and the buyer will only pay with a credit card, use an escrow service*—If a buyer has no other way of paying other than a credit card, suggest an escrow service. Make sure that the buyer picks up the extra escrow fee.

How to Use an Escrow Service

You'll find that it's quite easy to use an escrow service. Here's how you do it.

After the buyer and seller have agreed to use the service, both have to sign up with the escrow service. Unless both sign up with the same service, it won't agree to act as a go-between.

After both sign up for the service, one person has to initiate the transaction. It doesn't really matter whether the buyer or seller initiates it. Remember that whoever initiates the transaction, the buyer will always directly pay the escrow service, including the escrow fee. The person initiates the transaction by filling out a form that includes the email addresses of both the buyer and seller, a description of the item for sale, the purchase price of the item, and an agreed-upon inspection period, among other details.

If the buyer doesn't notify the escrow service of a problem within the inspection period, the escrow service automatically pays the seller. Pictured next is part of the form used to initiate an escrow transaction on the *www.iescrow.com* escrow site.

What's an inspection period?

The inspection period is the amount of time after the goods are received that the buyer has to notify the escrow service if there's a problem with the transaction.

Here's how you begin the process of using an escrow service for an auction transaction. This is the form used at the www.iescrow.com site.

Once the transaction is created, the buyer pays the service. The seller is told via email that the service has been paid and ships the goods. The goods have to be shipped insured (sometimes the escrow service includes insurance as part of its payment, and sometimes it won't), and the seller also has to have a tracking number for the item so that the shipment can be tracked.

After the buyer receives the goods, he has the agreed-upon inspection time in which to inspect the goods. If there's a problem with them, he tells the escrow service via email and ships the goods back to the seller. The seller doesn't get paid. If there's no problem with them, the escrow service pays the seller.

Escrow services may refuse to act as a go-between when certain goods are sold

Escrow services have rules about in which transactions they won't participate. Each has different rules, so check with your particular escrow service to see its rules.

Comparing the Top Escrow Services

There are a number of different escrow services you can use, each with their own fee structure and rules. The following sections provide a rundown on each—use this guide to help you decide which one is best for you.

i-Escrow

Your escrow costs may vary

The escrow costs covered here were accurate as of the time this book went to press. However, they may have changed since then, so check the sites for details.

i-Escrow at *www.iescrow.com* is one of the better-known escrow services because of its relationship with eBay. eBay users will probably want to use this service rather than others, if only because of how well integrated it is into eBay. Registered eBay users are automatically registered with i-Escrow, so that cuts out the registration step. Additionally, there are links right on auction pages that allow eBay users to create escrow transactions.

The service charges a minimum fee of $2.95 if a credit card is used (the minimum fee is $5.95 if payment is made in another way). The following table shows the additional fees charged based on the value of the purchased items.

Value of Item	Additional Fee
Up to $500	6% of the purchase price
$500–$2,500	$30 plus 5% of the purchase price over $500
$2,500–$5,000	$130 plus 4% of the purchase

I-Escrow currently doesn't handle transactions of over $5,000. These fees all refer to if a credit card is used; for fees when a card isn't used, check the site. The i-Escrow site is shown in the following figure.

TradeSafe

TradeSafe (*www.tradesafe.com*) is another popular escrow service. For items sold for up to $2,500, it charges a fee of five percent of the selling price. If a credit card is used, there's a minimum fee of $1.99. (For other methods of payment, the fee is three percent of the selling price.) For items sold for between $2,500 and $5,000, the fee is 4.5 percent of the selling price if a credit card is used, and 2.25 percent if another payment method is used. For items sold for more than $5,000, the fee is $113 plus one percent of the selling price. The site won't accept credit card payments for items sold for over $5,000.

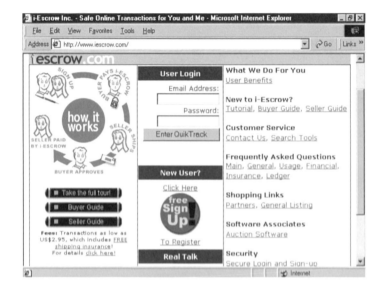

i-Escrow is the best place for eBay auctioneers to go for escrow services because it's integrated directly into eBay.

TradeSafe, like some other escrow services, has a handy escrow calculator, where you can enter the amount of the transaction and it automatically calculates a fee, so you easily know ahead of time what the fee will be. This calculator is shown in the following figure.

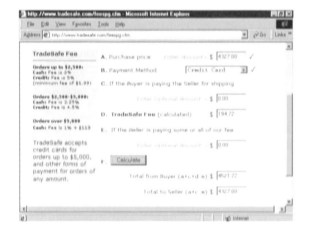

TradeSafe makes it easy to calculate your escrow payment with its online escrow calculator.

Trade-Direct

Trade-Direct, at *www.trade-direct.com*, has a minimum fee of $5, and charges a fee of 5 percent of the cost of the item up to $1,500 if paying by credit card, and 4 percent of the item over $1,500 if paying by credit card. If another payment method is used, the percentages are instead 3 and 2 percent. For amounts over $3,000, check the site for details.

Going, Going, Gone!

There are a number of reasons why you might want to use escrow services when buying or selling at auction sites. The following is what you need to know about using these services:

- Buyers should use escrow services when they're buying a big-ticket item or collectibles, or when they're buying from a seller who has a mixed feedback rating on an auction site.

- For the seller, an escrow service is useful if the buyer can only pay via credit card. Some escrow services also arrange for shipping insurance.

- To use an escrow service, both buyer and seller have to register at the site. Then one or the other fills out a form starting the transaction. No matter who creates the transaction, the buyer pays the escrow service directly.

- While it's customary for the buyer to pay all escrow fees, a buyer and seller can make other arrangements to have the seller pay some or all of the escrow fee.

- After the buyer pays the escrow service, the goods are shipped to him by the seller. He has a specified amount of time to inspect the goods, after which the escrow service pays the seller. If there are problems, the buyer ships the item back to the seller, and gets his money back. If there are no problems, the service pays the seller for the goods.

CHAPTER 22

Using Appraisal Firms, Verification Services, and Insurance

One of the biggest worries that new bidders have on auction sites is whether they'll be taken for a ride—they'll pay money to the seller and then never get the goods delivered, or, when the goods are delivered, they'll be damaged or not what was promised. This is especially true when the items are rare ones, such as rare coins, autographs, and similar items.

In this chapter, you'll learn the ways you can protect yourself from these kinds of problems. You'll learn how to use auction insurance for items under about $200 or so. For expensive collectibles, I'll show you how appraisal firms and verification services can be used at auctions so that buyers can be sure they're getting the real goods, not counterfeits.

How to Use Insurance on Auction Sites

To put bidders' minds at ease and protect them from fraud, some top auction sites, such as eBay and Amazon, offer auction insurance. You don't need to apply or pay extra for this kind of insurance. It automatically covers you when you bid and buy on the site, with certain limitations, as I'll explain later in this chapter.

Not all sites offer insurance. (For example, while eBay and Amazon both offer auction insurance, Yahoo Auctions doesn't, as of this writing.) The way that insurance works varies from site to site as well. It's important that, before bidding, you check to see whether the auction site carries insurance, and if it does, how it works. The following is a list of what you need to know about auction insurance before you bid:

What You'll Learn in This Chapter

▶ How to check out insurance policies on auction sites.

▶ How to file insurance claims.

▶ The difference between authentication, appraisal, and grading.

▶ How to use authentication, appraisal, and grading services.

▶ Where to go to get information about authentication, appraisal, and grading services.

- *Find out the amount of the coverage*—The amount that insurance covers varies from site to site. On eBay, for example, you're covered for up to $200 with a $25 deductible. That means you'll be out the first $25—eBay won't pay it. On Amazon, by contrast, coverage is up to $250 with no deductible.

Use an escrow service for amounts higher than insurance covers

Because insurance only covers up to $200 or $250, depending on the auction site, if you want to be safe when bidding on higher-ticket items, use an escrow service.

- *Learn how much time you have to file a claim*—This varies quite a bit from site to site. On eBay, for example, you have to register a complaint within 30 days of the auction's close. On Amazon, by contrast, you have to *wait* until 30 days after the auction closes to file a claim—you can't file a claim before then.

- *Read the terms of the insurance carefully*—Fine print accompanies all insurance policies, including those that cover online auctions. You'll find that insurance won't cover all items being auctioned on a site. On eBay, for example, insurance only applies if both buyer and seller have net positive feedback. The buyer is only allowed to file one claim a month. On Amazon, the seller has to have a positive feedback rating of at least 3.0, Dutch auctions aren't covered, and buyers have a lifetime limit of filing three claims.

How to File an Insurance Claim

A few items not covered by eBay insurance

The insurance offered by eBay covers only items that are allowed to be sold on the site. Among the items not covered are tobacco, firearms, and alcohol.

If you've been burned, you'll have to file a claim with the auction site to get your money back. Depending on the procedures of the site, it can take several months to get your money. The following bullets show how to file on Amazon and on eBay:

- *On Amazon*—You simply fill out a form with your contact information and your complaint. You have to wait 30 days after the auction closes. Amazon will investigate, and, if it finds you've been defrauded, you'll be sent payment within 14 days of when you file the claim. The claim form is shown in the following figure. To file the claim, click the Auction Guarantee area of Amazon auctions, and then click the Guarantee Claim Form.

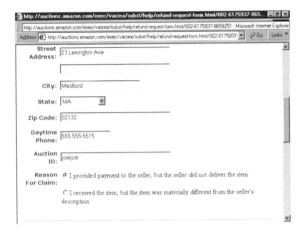

Here's how you'll make a claim to collect auction insurance on Amazon.

- *On eBay*—The process is more complicated on eBay and takes a much longer time before you'll get payment. (Because of this, I won't go into all the details here. Check the site for more.) Register your complaint with eBay's Fraud Reporting System within 30 days of when the auction closes. Get there by clicking Services from the main eBay page, clicking Safe Harbor, Insurance, and then following the directions. The information on that page will walk you through the entire claims process.

Auction insurance doesn't cover items damaged during shipping

Auction insurance doesn't cover items damaged during shipping. If the item is damaged during shipping, it's up to the seller and the buyer to decide how to handle the problem.

Appraisal, Authentication, and Grading Services

If you're buying a valuable collectible online, such as rare coins, stamps, autographs, or even rare baseball cards, you won't be able to examine the merchandise before buying. This can lead to big problems for the bidder—how do you know that you can trust the seller to be selling truly rare merchandise, or to honestly report the condition of the goods?

The way around the problem is to use one of a variety of appraisal services. These services employ objective experts who will verify the authenticity of collectibles and appraise and grade them. There are actually four different, related services the firms perform:

- *Authentication*—Determines whether a collectible is genuine, authentic, and is accurately described. An authenticator will be able to say, for example, whether a baseball supposedly signed by Babe Ruth is in fact, the real thing.

Verification services are different from authentication services

If you're buying collectibles or rare items, you may come across something called a verification service. Verification services are slightly different than authentication services. A verification service will confirm the identity of an item and evaluate its condition. These services are often used to track the history of ownership of an object, and sometimes use DNA tagging to do so. For example, a verification service will not only verify that a ball was signed by Babe Ruth, it will also verify who its previous owners were as well, so the history of the ball can be traced.

- *Grading*—A way of objectively evaluating the physical condition of something, such as "poor" or "mint condition." There are different grading systems for different kinds of items, such as coins, stamps, and trading cards. For example, trading cards range in grade from A1 to F1. Coins range in grade from poor to perfect uncirculated.

- *Appraisal services*—Estimate the value of an item, based on the items condition, authenticity, rarity, and the demand for it.

How to Use Appraisal and Grading Services

In general, appraisal and grading services aren't used by the buyer—instead, they're used by the seller. It would be awkward and maybe impossible for a potential buyer to have the items being auctioned off appraised and graded during the auction, especially because so many people bid on an item, and auctions only last for a brief amount of time.

It's a good idea to use more than one appraisal service

Experts may differ on the authenticity, condition, and value of an item. It's often a good idea to get more than one expert to appraise and grade an item.

Rather, the seller pays a service to appraise and grade an item *before* the auction starts. Then in the auction itself, the seller can say who appraised and graded the item and detail what the report said. This helps the seller beyond verification, it also helps the seller determine what price to set for the item. A seller, by himself, may not be able to determine the true value of a rare coin, but an appraisal service can.

Typically, a seller will ship the item to be appraised to a service. The service will then appraise the item and issue a report. Many services will encapsulate the item in plastic to protect it and put a label on it with details about the grading and authenticity of the item. The following figure shows a picture of a coin to which that's been done.

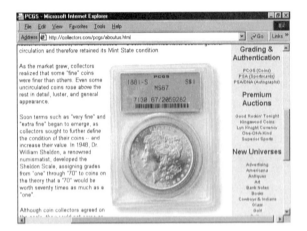

Here's an example of a coin that's been appraised, encapsulated in plastic, and labeled to show its grade.

The seller should show a clear picture of the graded, encapsulated item on the auction page and detail how the item has been graded.

Where to Find Appraisal and Grading Services

After you've decided to use an appraisal service, you need to find one. There are many you can use, and many of them specialize in one specific kind of item. The following sections discuss popular services and how to reach them.

International Society of Appraisers

www.isa-appraisers.org

This organization of appraisers will help you find an appraiser near you. You can search for an appraiser directly from the Web site, or you can call (888) 472-5587. Appraisers from the society have expertise in over 200 areas in four main categories: antiques and residential contents, fine art, gems and jewelry, and machinery and equipment.

Professional Coin Grading Service (PCGS)

www.pcgs.com

If you have coins that you need graded, here's the place to go. You'll find information about the service, as well as how to get your coins graded, from the site.

Professional Sports Authenticator (PSA)

psacard.com

If you have rare baseball cards, here's where to get information on how to get them authenticated. You'll find information about services from the site. Note that the site doesn't authenticate other sports memorabilia—it only handles cards. The following figure shows the PSA Web site.

Professional Sports Authenticator: Here's where to go to get rare baseball cards authenticated.

PSA/DNA

www.psadna.com

If you need an autograph authenticated, here's where to send it. The firm is run by PSA, but it authenticates other kinds of autographs, not just sports autographs. After it authenticates the autograph, it also uses DNA tagging so that the autograph can be traced from owner to owner.

Going, Going, Gone!

Among the best ways to make sure that you don't get taken for a ride at an auction site is to check the site's insurance policies and to use appraisal firms and verification services. The following is a summary of what you should know about them.

- Check your auction site to see whether it offers insurance. Read the rules closely, because not all insurance covers all items up for sale on the site. Generally, you'll be limited to coverage for items up to $200 or so.

- Carefully check the amount of time you have to file a claim for insurance reimbursement. For example, you have to file within 30 days after the close of the action on eBay, while, on Amazon, you have to *wait* 30 days after the end of the auction before you can apply.

- Sellers should use appraisal, grading, and authentication services on rare items so that they can assure bidders that the items are authentic and of the condition of the item. The services will also help the seller determine a minimum selling price.

PART 6

Appendixes

APPENDIX A

Auction Web Site Directory

There's a world of auctions beyond eBay—hundreds, probably thousands, of sites hold auctions every day online. In this appendix, you'll get listings of many of the top auction sites on the Internet, by category. Using everything you've learned in this book, you can visit the sites, bid and sell, make money, and have some fun.

General Auction Sites

If you're looking to buy everything from collectibles to cars to bubble wrap to software, go to one of the general auction sites listed here. In some instances, such as the giant auction site eBay, you'll find more items for sale in a particular category than even in the specialized auction sites.

Amazon Auctions

www.amazon.com, click Auctions

The most successful selling site on the Internet turns to auctions. Good, popular, all-around auction site.

AuctionAddict.com

www.auctionaddict.com

Good auction site for a wide variety of goods. Offers free auction listings for sellers; sellers only pay if their goods sell.

Auction Universe

www.auctionuniverse.com

Good, popular, all-around auction site. It offers free basic listings for sellers and low-cost extras, such as 25 cents for bold-faced listings. Sellers only pay if their goods sell.

Bid.com

www.bid.com

Big, popular auction site; you buy directly from the site itself, not from individuals.

eBay

www.ebay.com

The mother of all auction sites. If something can be bought or sold, you'll find it here.

Excite Auctions

http://auctions.excite.com

The popular search site has an auction area. Busy, with a wide variety of items for sale.

First Auction

www.firstauction.com

You buy directly from the auction site here. Of all the sites where you buy directly from the auction site, this has the widest variety of kinds of goods for sale.

Haggle.com

www.haggle.com

There's no fee here for basic listings; sellers only pay if their items sell. The site focuses mainly on computer equipment, but also has other items for sale.

uBid

www.ubid.com

You buy from the auction site itself. Sells primarily computer equipment, housewares, sporting equipment, and jewelry.

Yahoo! Auctions

http://*auctions.yahoo.com*, click Auctions

The most popular search site on the Internet has a big, popular auction area. Very active; lots on sale.

Computers, Software, and Electronics

There are countless auctions that specialize in computers, software, and electronics. Many are auctions in which you buy directly from the site itself, although there are also a good number of person-to-person sites that specialize in computer auctions. The following sections list many of the best computer and software auction sites online.

Auction Warehouse

www.auctionwarehouse.com

You buy straight from the auction site rather than from individuals here. It includes some home and leisure products as well as computers and electronics.

Egghead Auctions

www.surplusauctions.com

The onetime software and computer store now operates sites in cyberspace, including an auction site. You buy directly from the site itself, and you'll find a lot of stuff on sale.

Onsale.com

www.onsale.com

Here you buy from the auction site itself. In addition to computer equipment, software, and electronics, this auction site sells sporting goods.

OutPost Auctions

www.outpostauctions.com

This is an auction site run by the computer and software buying site *Outpost.com*. Good selection here.

ZDNet Auctions

www.zdnetauctions.com

Excellent site for person-to-person computer auctions. Hardware, software, electronics, gaming... there's a big selection here. Domain names are even up for sale at this popular computer auction site.

Collectibles and Antiques

The online auction craze has been fueled, in good part, by the ability to buy collectibles easily from people around the world. Whether it's Pez dispensers, Beanie Babies, autographs, or any other kind of collectible, there's a specialized site. The following sections list a selection of sites selling collectibles and antiques.

Antique Trails

www.antique-trails.com

This site offers collectibles of every kind, along with other items. There's no charge to sellers for listing their items.

Auction Autograph

www.auctionautograph.com

At this auction are autographs of all kinds, ranging from the grade B-movie movie actor Christopher Lee to the golfer Fuzzy Zoeller.

AuctionPort

www.auctionport.com

The site specializes in antiques and collectibles, but has other items for sale as well.

Biddington's Auction Galleries

www.biddingtons.com

You'll find antiques and collectibles as well as fine art for sale here.

Christie's

www.christies.com

The famous auction house that sells everything from Marilyn Monroe dresses to ancient Asian art to artifacts from the U.S.

space program now has on online auction site (see the following figure).

From outer space items to Marilyn Monroe dresses to Asian art—you'll find that and more at Christie's online.

Collectors Auction

www.collectorsauction.com

A big site with all kinds of collectibles, from coins to cigars to dolls, records, wine, stamps, and most any other collectible you can think of.

eHammer

www.ehammer.com

A good-sized site where you can find antiques and collectibles.

The Real Hollywood Online Auction

www.unistudiosauction.com

If you want to bid on original tickets to the *I Love Lucy* show, Barbara Streisand's napkin holder, Dorothy Lamour's evening gloves, a license plate owned by Elvis Presly, and similar items, come to this auction site run by Universal Studios.

The Serious Collector

www.seriouscollector.com

There are collectibles of all sorts as well as antiques for sale here. In addition to an auction area, there's also a place where you can buy items at a preset price with no bidding.

Sotheby's

www.sothebys.com

The world-famous auction site has come to the Internet with expensive antiques and high-end collectibles of every kind, from Allen Ginsberg manuscripts to baseball memorabilia.

Teletrade

www.teletrade.com

Coins, sports cards, memorabilia, fine art, movie posters… there's a big range of collectibles on sale here. It's a "live" auction format where you bid in real time against others.

Coins and Stamps

Coins and stamps have always had a sizable number of collectors, and it's no great surprise that there are many excellent coin and stamp auctions available online. Check out the following choices.

Coin Universe

www.coin-universe.com

In addition to buying and selling coins here, you'll also find articles and resources for coin collectors.

Jake's Online Coin Auction

www.jakescoinauction.com

If you're interested in bidding on coins, check in here. You'll find a big selection of coins, ranging from inexpensive to rare.

Sandafayre

www.sandafayre.com

Big stamp auction site, filled with a large number of high-quality stamps.

Stamp Auctions

www.stampauctions.com

This site specializes in auctions of stamps from around the world, from Aden to Zanzibar.

Beanie Babies and Toys

Toys and Beanie Babies aren't just child's play. They're big business online. If you're a collector or seller of Beanies or toys—or want to be one—check out the following sites.

Action Figure Auctions

www.actionfigureauctions.com

Don't expect run-of-the-mill action figures at this auction. Instead, you'll find things such as Ozzy Osborne action figures, Austin Powers action figures, and similar oddball items, as you can see in the next figure.

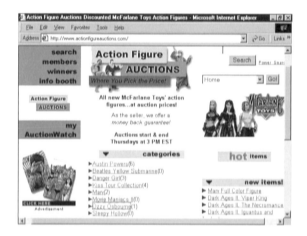

If you're looking for oddball action figures, you'll find them for sale at auction at www.actionfigure-auctions.com.

Beanie Time Auction

www.beanietime.com

All Beanies, all the time. Need I say more?

Just Beanies

www.justbeanies.com

Just as the site's name says: All you'll find here for auction are Beanie Babies.

Replay Toys Collectible Toy Auction

www.replaytoys.com

You'll find toys ranging from early G.I. Joe to current Star Wars, Barbies, and everything in between for auction here. The biggest focus is on dolls and action figures.

Sports Cards and Memorabilia

When you were a kid, sports cards were things to be traded among friends, or flipped for, and an autograph was something you tried to get from a player at batting practice before a game. No longer. They're the province of collectors now. The following are some of the card collecting and sports memorabilia auction sites you'll find on the Internet.

Curran's Cards and Auctions

www.curranscards.com

Thousands of sports cards of every kind you can imagine—a big site full of great cards.

fan2fan Sports Auction

www.fan2fan.com

This site specializes in sports cards, so whether it's a Mantle & Berra card, Mario Lemieux, or Michael Jordan you're after, you'll find something here.

SportsAuction

www.sportsauction.com

Autographed sports memorabilia plus cards and other kinds of sports collectibles.

SportsTrade

www.sportstrade.com

Autographs, plus autographed jerseys, balls, and other sports memorabilia are at auction here.

Helpful Sites about Auction

Helpful for anyone interested in online auctions are sites that will help you be a better bidder or buyer or help you find auctions more easily. The following sites will help you do all that.

AuctionRover

www.auctionrover.com

An excellent auction site that offers an extremely good AuctionBot that will search many auction sites for you and show you items up for sale at all of them. In addition to that, the site will also host your auction image files, and there's a list of auction sites and helpful auction information and advice.

AuctionWatch

www.auctionwatch.com

A great site for those interested in auctions. There's auction news, tips, advice, insider information, and links to hundreds of auction sites. This site has an auction robot for searching many different auction sites as well.

Bidder's Edge

www.biddersedge.com

Instead of visiting dozens of different auction sites, stop here and shop them all. It's a kind of auction robot in which you can search many different auction sites simultaneously for items you want to bid on. The Bidder's Edge Web site is shown in the following figure.

Internet Auction List

www.internetauctionlist.com

For a comprehensive set of links to auctions of every type—both online and in the real world—head here and start clicking.

Search many different auction sites for the items you want to buy from www.biddersedge.com.

APPENDIX B

Glossary

AuctionBot   A Web site, such as *www.biddersedge.com* and *www.auctionwatch.com*, that searches through many auction sites and reports on the items up for sale on them.

Auction insurance   Insurance provided by sites such as eBay and Amazon, so that if a buyer is burned at an auction, the auction site will reimburse him.

Auction listing   The page that describes an item up for auction, including all the relevant information—prices, bidding, buyer and seller information, and more.

Auction relisting   A new listing for an item that was previously listed but did not sell.

Auctioneer   Another term for the seller at an e-auction.

Bid   The act of offering a price on an item up for auction (I bid on a painting), or a way of describing the offer itself (My bid was $100).

Bidder   A person who makes a bid on an item in an auction.

Bidding history   A listing of all the bids placed on a particular auction.

Bidding increment   The amount by which a bid must be raised for a bidder to beat the previous bid.

Bid shielding   A practice in which someone makes an artificially high bid to scare away other bidders and then retracts the bid so that the retracter's compatriot can buy the item at a low price.

Collectibles   Items that collectors crave and bid on. These can be anything from Pez dispensers to baseball cards to Depression-era glass.

Dutch auction   An auction in which several items are offered for sale at the same time and in which a certain number of bidders will all win the auction at the same price.

Escrow service   A service that serves as a go-between for the buyer and seller at an auction. The buyer pays the escrow service, which holds the money until the goods have been delivered; at that point, the escrow service pays the seller.

Featured auction   An auction given special placement and prominence on an auction site, such as on the front page. Often, a seller has to pay extra to have his item become a featured item.

Feedback   The comments that bidders and sellers at auction sites make about other bidders and sellers.

Flash auction   An auction conducted in real time—that is, the bidding takes place live, usually over a short period of time.

GIF   One of the computer file formats that can be used for a graphic posted in a Web page or on an auction site.

High bidder   The person who offers the highest bid at an auction and so is awarded the item.

HTML (Hypertext Markup Language)   A language used to create pages on the World Wide Web. A browser interprets HTML commands and displays the results on Web pages.

Insertion fee   See *listing fee*.

Item details page   See *auction listing*.

JPEG   One of the formats that graphics have to be in so they can be posted on Web pages.

Listing fee   The fee an auction site charges a seller for the initial auction listing. It's usually based on the minimum bid set by the seller.

Minimum selling price   A price set by the seller, which is the minimum price at which the bidding can start. (See also *reserve price auction*.)

Money order   A special type of check, most often purchased from the U.S. Postal Service, that can be used in place of cash for payment.

Online auction   An auction conducted on the Internet.

Person-to-person auction   An auction in which you buy from another person instead of from the auction site. eBay, Yahoo!, and Amazon auctions are examples of sites that specialize in person-to-person auctions.

Proxy bidding   A type of bidding in which a "proxy" automatically makes bids for people, based on their highest-specified bid. The proxy bids the minimum *bidding increment* above the next-highest bidder, automatically keeps making bids until the highest-specified bid is reached, and then makes no more bids.

Private auction   An auction in which the bidder's identities aren't revealed.

Reserve price auction   An auction in which items will only be sold when a minimum reserve price is met. The seller sets the minimum reserve price before the auction begins.

Restricted access auction   An auction in which only adults are allowed to enter and bid. Frequently, these auctions involve erotica or other adult material.

Search engine   An Internet site that searches the rest of the Internet and reports to you on what it finds based on your input keywords.

Seller   A person at an auction site who offers an item up for sale.

Shill bidding   A practice in which the seller or a friend of the seller bids on the item in an attempt to artificially drive up the selling price.

Shipping costs   The price of shipping the item to the buyer. Typically, the buyer pays shipping costs.

Sniping   The act of making the highest bid at the last possible moment so that no one else has a chance to make a higher bid.

Tags   The codes used by HTML that tell a browser how to display Web pages.

Title   A description of an auction that appears on the most prominent part of an auction listing and that also appears when people browse through the categories on an auction site.

Web server   A special computer on the Internet that holds and delivers information, such as Web pages.

Winning bid   The highest bid at the end of an auction, as long as the highest bid is at least as high as the reserve price set by the seller, if a reserve price has been set.

INDEX

Tell Us What You Think!

As the reader of this book, you are our most important critic and commentator. We value your opinion and want to know what we're doing right, what we could do better, what areas you'd like to see us publish in, and any other words of wisdom you're willing to pass our way.

You can email or write me directly to let me know what you did or didn't like about this book—as well as what we can do to make our books stronger.

Please note that I cannot help you with technical problems related to the topic of this book, and that due to the high volume of mail I receive, I might not be able to reply to every message.

When you write, please be sure to include this book's title and author as well as your name and phone or number. I will carefully review your comments and share them with the author and editors who worked on the book.

Email: *internet_sams@mcp.com*

Mail: Mark Taber
            Associate Publisher
            Sams Publishing
            201 West 103rd Street
            Indianapolis, IN 46290 USA

SAMS
Teach Yourself
Today

Sams Teach Yourself
e-Travel Today

Planning Vacations, Finding Bargains, and Booking Reservations Online

Mark Orwoll
ISBN: 0-672-31822-9
$17.99 US/$26.95 CAN